Will Dobbie has produced
examining God's plan and e
Everlasting works through t
skill that is bound to bring in

Derek W. H. Thomas

Senior Minister, First Presbyterian Church, Columbia SC; Teaching Fellow, Ligonier Ministries; Chancellor's Professor, Reformed Theological Seminary

Biblical truth is designed to illuminate the mind, soften the heart and energise the will. All three elements are here in abundance in Will Dobbie's insightful and motivating exposition of the great foundations of Christian faith and experience.

Combining profound theology with practical everyday-life applications, it also includes vivid contemporary illustrations and answers a variety of objections raised against the Bible's truth. Its thirty chapters, intended for daily devotions, are not to be read superficially. This is a manual and guide book for personal spiritual growth towards maturity and as such it needs to be inwardly digested and diligently applied. It will bring assurance and confidence to the believer, strength to the church and glory to God.

David Jackman
Past President, The Proclamation Trust, London

Many Christians wrongly think that reformed doctrine is dry, intellectual and unhelpfully divisive. These thirty daily devotions demonstrate that this is not the case. They provide a wonderfully God-centred understanding of our salvation, that is thoroughly biblical and fosters true humility, joy, assurance, hope and love for God and His glory. ... These devotions would be ideal for a young believer wanting to grow in the faith, or a mature believer who wants to have their heart warmed afresh by the glorious doctrines of grace.

John Stevens
National Director, Fellowship of Independent Evangelical Churches

You know those fresh, bright mornings? Maybe in October as the golden leaves fall, maybe in January as the frost tingles and sparkles, maybe in April as the whole earth seems to awaken, or in July when dawn's already warm with the hint of the glory to come?

That's what you hold in your hands. For each day of the month Will has given us a fresh, bright glimpse of God's glory. As clear as a dawn praising a wonderful day, his descriptions and explanations of deep bible truths will make you long for more of our great God. And when the grey, dreaded days come – and they will, they always do – then here is honest, hard-won treasure too, gathered in the sunshine but stored up for the cold.

This book will do you good, whatever kind of day you're facing.

Chris Green
Vicar, St James, Muswell Hill, London
Former Vice Principal, Oak Hill College, London

I was once given the advice, 'Read the small books by the big authors.' I get the sentiment. But something in me grates with talk of 'big authors.' I think I prefer the advice: 'Read good books by godly authors.' And this book is a good read by a godly guy. It's deep and devotional, whilst being concise and accessible. Ministering in a deprived context I'm always on the lookout for books that will help me communicate these eternal truths in simple ways. And this book is a massive help to that end.

Andy Prime
Author and pastor, 20schemes

...With pastoral wisdom and theological clarity, Will Dobbie walks us through all that God has done for us in Christ. This rich devotional guide to the 'order of salvation' will help you grow in knowledge of yourself and your God.

Jonty Rhodes
Minister, Christ Church Central, Leeds, UK

In an age of anxiety and uncertainty, this book helpfully fixes our eyes on God's unshakeable plan for every believer, stretching from His love in eternity past through to His secure promises for our future. Will writes with real clarity, serving us with doctrine that is always devotional, and in reading it I was reassured, excited, and moved to pray with gratitude and joy to our glorious God of wisdom and grace.

Martin Ayers
Rector of St Silas Church, Glasgow & author of *Keep the Faith* and *Naked God*

I love this book! Will Dobbie is thoroughly biblical, theologically robust, and immensely readable as he tracks us through the mountain country of life in union with King Jesus. Here is a devotional fit for daily feasting! Long hard chews on each chapter, as Dobbie unfolds the glories of a God who is 'mighty to save', will give the Christian a breath-taking view of all they possess in Christ.

Natalie Brand
Tutor for Women, Union School of Theology, Wales & author of several books, including *Prone to Wander* and *The Good Portion: Salvation*

FROM EVERLASTING TO EVERLASTING

Every Believer's Biography

WILL DOBBIE

CHRISTIAN
FOCUS

Copyright © Will Dobbie 2022

Paperback ISBN 978-1-5271-0837-0
Ebook ISBN   978-1-5271-0905-6

10 9 8 7 6 5 4 3 2 1

Published in 2022
by
Christian Focus Publications Ltd,
Geanies House, Fearn, Ross-shire,
IV20 1TW, Scotland, Great Britain.

www.christianfocus.com

Designed by James Amour

Printed by Bell & Bain, Glasgow

CONTENTS

Act IV – The Christian Life

Act V – The Life To Come

To Michelle
Fellow-pilgrim, best friend, soul-mate.

The Redeemer Croydon church family. Being your pastor was a life-changing privilege which gave rise to many good things, just one of which is this book. You were in mind on every page. Thank you for showing me what these truths look like lived out in community.

Benjamin Vrbicek. Brother, your selfless kindness and wisdom made all the difference in the early days of this project. Thank you.

Rosanna Burton and Anne Norrie at Christian Focus Publishing. Working with you both was a pleasure from start to finish. Thank you for your help and encouragement throughout.

Foreword

We lost my younger brother at the beach—just a toddler and learning to walk, he snuck away in a sea of people. Although I was his older brother, I was still too young to be either culpable for losing him or much help in finding him. Our family had just moved to England, where we would spend the next three years, and my mother wanted to take her sons on an outing to make memories adventuring in a new country. A couple of hours later, we found him holding the hand of an elderly woman as she walked up and down the beach looking for what she rightly assumed would be a frantic mother. That day my mother certainly made memories.

A similar incident happened to my family one summer at a water park, except this time *I* was the parent with the lost child—a father old enough to be more than culpable, yet still struggling to be any help in finding my daughter. She was only lost a dozen minutes or so, but it felt much longer. We found her near the lazy river.

I suspect most parents have a similar version of the same story, whether the child wandered off at a beach or amusement park, a sporting event or concert. Thankfully, almost all lost-child stories have happy endings that, in hindsight, parents can laugh about with their grown-up children.

As I read the Bible, I learn that not only does God save His people from their sins, but He also intends for Christians to *understand* their salvation: to understand that they were lost but now are found. Our practised belief in God's eternal plan to save us, to make us more like Him, and to one day make every wrong right, provides so much of a Christian's peace and joy in a world full of angst. This is not to say that when we are confused about aspects of our salvation we are necessarily any less saved, but it is to say that when we lack understanding of the riches of God's redemption, we will lack joy and, probably also, obedience.

This is why I was excited when Will first told me about his idea for a book that would trace the story of a believer's redemption from beginning to end. Now that Will has finished the book, I'm only more excited. The Christian world needs devotional material with both warm-hearted prose and theologically rich truth, not simply one or the other. Will's book *From Everlasting to Everlasting* has both.

As a pastor of a local church, I have another reason to long for others to read this book. In our day so many issues conspire to divide local churches that Christians need constant reminders of the one story that binds us irrevocably together. Just as a group of parents could share a meal together and bond as they tell each other stories of the common experience of losing and finding a child—the panic, the relief, the thanksgiving—so also I believe a church will bond together when we understand that every believer's biography is indeed **every** believer's biography.

In other words, I can, and should, preach to my church about the need for Christians to pursue the unity we already have in Christ, but my pleas for unity will accomplish little if, deep down, those in my church believe that which makes us different carries more weight than that which makes us the same. Biblically speaking, the opposite is true of Christians: the deep story of our sin and salvation, of Christ's cross and consummation, carries more weight than our lesser identities in gender, ethnicity, or any social status. 'How can I relate to her?' I might be tempted to think. 'We have nothing in common.' Except that when we have Christ in common, we have everything in common. As Paul writes in Galatians, 'For as many of you as were baptized into Christ have put on Christ. There is neither Jew nor Greek, there is neither slave nor free, there is no male and female, for you are all one in Christ Jesus' (Gal. 3:27-28). *From Everlasting to Everlasting* reminds us that Christians share common, gospel bedrock, a unity deeper and sturdier than mere affinities.

Your tour guide on this panorama of God's salvation knows all this too. And he's found a way to share it with you in thirty daily excursions through the vistas of our redemption. Some of the concepts

Will writes about may be new to you, while you may have heard others many times before. Regardless, my prayer for you is that God would use these words to pour fresh peace and joy into your life—that you would know in your inmost being, as Paul writes in Ephesians, 'what is the breadth and length and height and depth … [of] the love of Christ' (Eph. 3:18-19). I pray that this knowledge that we once were lost but now are found would bind us together, that we would unite over the common experience of the panic and the relief and the thanksgiving that comes when God washes our sins as white as snow.

BENJAMIN VRBICEK
Community Evangelical Free Church
Harrisburg, Pennsylvania

BENJAMIN VRBICEK is the lead pastor at Community Evangelical Free Church in Harrisburg, Pennsylvania and the managing editor for Gospel-Centered Discipleship. Benjamin and his wife, Brooke, have six children. He has authored several books, including *Struggle Against Porn* and *Don't Just Send a Resume*, and has also written for The Gospel Coalition, Desiring God, For The Church, 9Marks, and Christianity Today.

Introduction

Day 1

The God Who Saves:
The Order of Salvation

Think of a time you were lost.

I remember leading my isolated platoon deep in a maze of side streets in the Iraqi city of Amarah. Night was falling and we knew insurgents were close, intent on a kill or, possibly worse, a capture. I'll never forget the rising fear as it dawned on me that I had lost track of our exact location. I'll also never forget the relief when my map made sense again. We completed the patrol without casualties.

Or to change contexts wildly (bear with me – I was reading this story to my children just this morning), imagine what it was like for the Minotaur's victims, summoned to Crete every nine years by King Minos. I can see them creeping around the dark corridors of the disorienting Labyrinth, hearts pounding and ears straining for the terrifying man-bull stalking them.

One year that group included Theseus. In the Greek myth, King Minos' love-struck daughter slips him a ball of magic string as he enters the maze. The string unravels in front of him, leading him to where he can slay the monster before guiding him safely out again.

Our world can sometimes feel like a maze of side streets in enemy territory. Or the Labyrinth, with monsters lurking in shadowy corners, ready to pounce as we pass. As Jesus promised, 'In this world you will have trouble.'[1] In fact, sometimes the abuse, the death of a child, the

---

1. John 16:33 (NIV).

cancer, the debt, the state of the marriage, the loneliness, the depression, can make us wonder if Theseus had it easy with just a Minotaur.

And so we do our best. Side-streets, labyrinth – pick your analogy – but we try to navigate a world in which we may be ambushed at any turn, whether by our own self-destructive sin, the sin of others against us, Satan and his malevolent demons, or the tragedy-triggering fallenness of creation in general.

Of course, this portrayal of life isn't the full picture. Life can be full of laughter and happiness. In fact, for the person whose identity is in Christ, there is deep confidence and joy available in *all* circumstances. 'I have learned in *whatever* situation I am to be content' said the Apostle Paul.[2] But as a pastor, I look out over my congregation each Sunday and am reminded of the myriads of suffering and trouble that are part of the human condition. Joy and tears are not mutually exclusive. (Younger readers, if in doubt give it a few more years. You'll see what I mean.)

So what is to be our roadmap through the side streets, the string to guide us through the labyrinth, our source of direction in life?

The Bible's answer for us is a stage-by-stage roadmap from eternity past to eternity future. It's a pathway marked out for us by God consisting of multiple steps, some sequential and some simultaneous. No matter how wild or random life may seem, this is the trail along which He is leading us. It will ultimately guide us home to unimaginable joy.

In this devotional, we've selected thirty of the stages on this pathway. Think of them as aid stations lining the route of a marathon, or pitons hammered into a mountainside leading to the summit. They reassure us that we're on the right path and secure us along the way.

The core elements of this pathway are what theologians call the *Ordo Salutis* (Order of Salvation). The term *Ordo Salutis* was coined by Lutheran theologians in the mid-1720s, but the order by which God saves His people has always been on display in His Word. Christians have framed it in various ways, but we can outline it like this:

1. Election
2. Calling
3. Regeneration
4. Conversion

---

2. Philippians 4:11.

5. Justification
6. Reconciliation
7. Sanctification
8. Perseverance
9. Glorification

These truths form the spine of the thirty entries in this devotional. Don't worry if any of them are new or unclear to you. In the daily entries that follow, we'll be exploring what God's Word has to say about each. 'Great are the works of the Lord, studied by all who delight in them.'[3]

Note that while some of salvation's stages occur in the believer's life in turn, others happen simultaneously. However, even when we can't speak of a chronological sequence, there is still a causal, logical sequence presented by Scripture (for example in stages 2-6 above). When I backed my car into a neighbour's vehicle, the impact and the dent occurred simultaneously, yet the impact had to happen for the dent *then* to happen.

It's also worth noting that every stage of the journey on which we're about to embark is centred on Jesus Christ. It doesn't move us 'from' Christ or even 'to' Christ. Nor is Jesus a staging post at a point on the journey, like the cross or my conversion. Any part of the process is incoherent apart from Christ.

As J. I. Packer points out, 'the entire *Ordo Salutis* ... is bound to the mystical union with Christ. There is no gift that has not been earned by him.'[4] Calvin says likewise: 'So long as we are without Christ and separated from him, nothing which he suffered and did for the salvation of the human race is of the least benefit to us. To communicate to us the blessings which he received from the Father, he must become ours and dwell in us.'[5] If the *Ordo Salutis* is linear like a railway journey, with the different stages like stations along the

---

3. Psalm 111:2.

4. J. I. Packer, 'An Introduction to Covenant Theology' (2012). This is the introduction to Herman Witsius' *The Economy of the Covenants between God and Man: Comprehending A Complete Body of Divinity* (Nabu, 2010).

5. John Calvin, *The Institutes of the Christian Religion*, ed. John T. McNeill, trans. Ford L. Battles, 2 vols. (Louisville, KY: Westminster John Knox, 1960), 3.1.537.

route, Christ is the ever-present, unchanging and essential rails. In Paul's words, 'All the promises of God find their "Yes" in him [Jesus].'[6]

One final, practical note: the doctrines we're about to dive into are so deep and rich that I would recommend you allocate to each, if possible, not one but two days. Spiritual truths take time to sink into our hearts. I have tried to saturate my explanation of each doctrine in Scripture, and to provide avenues for further meditation in some of the footnotes. In the journey ahead, dwelling unhurriedly on each truth in turn will repay your patience.

Let's now allow God's Word to show us the order of His salvation. This will give us a deeper understanding of where we have been, where we are, and where we are going. It will open to us great reservoirs of comfort and confidence as well as a deeper knowledge of our Saviour, as we travel His pathway through this world and beyond. In the Psalmist's words, 'From everlasting to everlasting, you are God.'[7]

Welcome to your biography.

Prayer:

Sovereign God of order, in the midst of this turbulent world I praise you for the path of life. In the weeks ahead, allow me to come to know you, what you have done for me, and what you will do for me more deeply than ever before in my life. Grant me joy, confidence, comfort and deep, lasting life-change as a result. In the name of the Christ who is your power and wisdom, Amen.

Meditation:

2 Corinthians 4:18 says, 'We look not to the things that are seen but to the things that are unseen. For the things that are seen are transient, but the things that are unseen are eternal.' What things in your life right now might give the impression that the world is random and chaotic? Why would Satan love you to disbelieve or forget about a path through the storm?

---

6. 2 Corinthians 1:20.

7. Psalm 90:2.

Act I
Life Plans

Day 2

The God Who Agrees: The Eternal Covenant

One of the glories of our salvation is that it was established in eternity past by God's sovereign choice of His people. But in the bottomless depths of that eternity, other realities were moving as well – a 'deeper magic' as Aslan might say. They're little known and often under-appreciated but immensely rich and scriptural. Before God elected us, He foreknew us. And even before He foreknew us, He covenanted with Himself to redeem us.[1] This is known as the Covenant of Redemption or the Eternal Covenant.

In this covenant, the members of the Trinity each pledged different roles.

The Father agreed to give the Son a people for His own possession. Jesus knew this when He prayed, 'Father, glorify me in your own presence with the glory that I had with you before the world existed. I have manifested your name to the people whom you gave me out of the world. Yours they were, and you gave them to me.'[2]

When my father promised to take me fishing as a boy, I would take that to include everything necessary for it to be fulfilled – drive us to the river, help set up my equipment, bring lunch and so on. The Father's promise of a people for His Son entailed many profound, beautiful actions, all of which He fulfilled.[3]

---

1. This sequence is logical rather than sequential as it took place in eternity past, before time had been created. See the Introduction.

2. John 17:5, 6. See also John 17:2, 9, 24; Luke 22:29.

3. This included: planning the cross for the Son (Rev. 13:8), promising the Son (Gen. 3:15), preparing the way for the Son (Mark 1:2,3), sending the Son (John 3:16), endorsing the Son (Matt. 3:17), guiding the Son (Luke 6:12), giving the

19

The Son for His part agreed to redeem His people in obedient accordance with His Father's plan. 'For I have come down from heaven, not to do my own will but the will of him who sent me.'[4] 'This charge [of dying and rising] I have received from my Father.'[5] Like the Father, the Son's agreement also entailed many extraordinary things, all of which He faithfully fulfilled.[6]

The explicitly named parties in the Eternal Covenant are the Father and Son. Some have argued that the apparent absence of the Spirit here undermines the Trinity. However, the members of the Trinity don't act independently of each other. They are perfectly, constantly unified. In Augustine's words, 'just as Father and Son and Holy Spirit are inseparable, so they work inseparably.'[7]

Furthermore, the Spirit's characteristic nature is to point away from Himself, directing our focus to the Father and the Son.[8] In Scripture, His role is to enact and apply the will of the Father and the Son while normally remaining tacit. For example, it is He who applies the saving work of the Son to the people promised by the Father.[9] We can be confident that the entire Trinity is operating in the Eternal Covenant.

One key implication of God's Eternal Covenant is this: it displays His aseity. In other words, it displays the self-sufficiency of His existence, independent of anything outside Himself.[10]

Son words (John 17:8), giving the Son authority (John 17:2), delivering the Son for death (Acts 4:28), raising the Son (Rom. 4:25), receiving back the Son (John 14:28), accepting the Son's request to send the Spirit (John 14:16), and accepting the Son's ongoing advocacy for His people (1 John 2:1,2). This list isn't comprehensive, but the point is that the Father completed the many things included within His promise.

4. John 6:38.

5. John 10:18.

6. The Son obeying His Father's will entailed: entering the world with a human body (Col. 2:9) and nature (Phil. 2:6-8), being subject to God's law (Gal. 4:4), fulfilling and accomplishing the law (Matt. 5:17,18), taking His people's guilt (Isa. 53:6), paying their penalty (Isa. 53:5), having His righteousness credited to them (2 Cor. 5:21), drawing them to Himself (John 12:32), and having laid His life down, taking it up again (John 10:18).

7. Augustine, 'De Trinitate' (New City Press, 1991), 1.7. This is known as the concept of inseparable operations.

8. John 15:26; 16:13, 14.

9. John 6:38, 39; 17:4.

10. Acts 17:25

'Then Moses said to God, "If ... they ask me, 'What is his name?' what shall I say to them?" God said to Moses, "I AM WHO I AM."'[11] Somewhat randomly at first sight, God speaks these words out of a bush which is on fire yet fails to burn up. Yet this is a brilliant (if you'll forgive the pun) visual illustration of the very aseity He is communicating to Moses. Unlike humans, the Creator's own existence blazes perpetually, of its own accord, without ever being depleted or needing fuel or going out.

In the winter months, as a family, we love to eat by candlelight in the evenings. But the candles burn only because we light them. And then as the days go by, they gradually shorten until they're tiny stumps which eventually, inevitably go out. This is exactly what our lives are like. This is part of what it means to be human. God is different. Being Himself the First Cause, His existence is without a prior cause. His life blazes self-sufficiently, independently and perpetually. He is 'a se'.

So what? Is this merely abstract theology or is there a practical point for us? And what does God's aseity have to do with the Eternal Covenant anyway? These are deep theological foundations we are digging to be sure, but be patient. The down-to-earth, life-changing truths they support, which we have nearly reached, are worth theological and intellectual sweat! Here comes the final spade-work before we get to see how this impacts our day-to-day lives.

The Eternal Covenant shows God's aseity in the following way. By it, He expresses His innate qualities without having to depend on creation to do so. Qualities like His glory, love, wisdom, faithfulness, relational nature and so on require situations of more than one solitary party in order to exist. The trinitarian God fulfils this requirement within Himself, without having to rely on creation's existence, because He, uniquely, is multi-personal.

Other monadic, single-person gods such as Allah have to depend on creation in order to express their glory, love, wisdom and so on. In other words, they are not self-sufficient. They are contingent on creation for being themselves. They are fundamentally incomplete and needy. Compared to the living God, they are one-dimensional. In the

---

11. Exodus 3:13-14.

one true God, as C. S. Lewis says, 'there is no hunger that needs to be filled, only plenteousness that desires to give'.[12] Lewis goes on,

> We must keep always before our eyes that vision of Lady Julian's in which God carried in His hand a little object like a nut, and that nut was 'all that is made.' God who needs nothing, loves into existence wholly superfluous creatures in order that He may love and perfect them.[13]

So why has God chosen to show us His aseity through His Eternal Covenant? So what? Here is the practical fruit for us from the theological foundations laid above.

The Eternal Covenant displays His innate glory, as each person's qualities play out before one another.[14] It is only as an innately glorious God that He is able to display His glory before His people.[15] His glory is not derived and fake. It is inherent, and more real and precious than anything else in your life. In approaching Him, you come not to a cardboard cut-out god but to the meaning of life Himself. You are coming to glory Himself. With this God alone, you get to be part of something greater than yourself.

The Eternal Covenant displays His innate love, as the members of the Trinity relate to each other in love.[16] It is only as an innately loving God that He is able to reach out and love His people.[17] The triune God has placed His love, better than life itself, upon you.[18] With this God you are more loved than you will ever fathom, for ever and ever and ever. No matter what your life's circumstances, you can know that you are complete.

The Eternal Covenant displays His innate wisdom, as the members of the Trinity collaborate and coordinate plans of infinite magnitude between themselves.[19] It is only as an innately wise God that He is able to work His wisdom for His people's everlasting joy in

---

12. C. S. Lewis, *The Four Loves* (Harcourt, 1960), p. 126.
13. ibid., p. 127.
14. John 17:5.
15. Romans 11:36.
16. John 17:24.
17. John 3:16.
18. Psalm 63:3.
19. 1 Corinthians 2:9.

Him.[20] The God of infinite intelligence and knowledge has planned for your eternal happiness and fulfilment in Him. You can know that the logistics of your security and joy in this world, as well as in the world to come, are covered.

The Eternal Covenant displays His innate faithfulness, as the members of the Trinity commit to and fulfil their promised roles from across the expanse of eternity, at unfathomable cost.[21] It is only as an innately faithful God that He is able to reach out and anchor His people's salvation in His own faithful nature.[22] Your salvation is as sure as the strength of the Father's and Son's and Spirit's bonds with each other. You can walk through this world with utter confidence in your eternal future.

The Eternal Covenant displays His innate relational nature, as each member of the Trinity interacts with the others in eternity past.[23] It is only as an innately relational God that He is able to reach out for a personal connection with you.[24] Before you existed, He knew you by name. He enjoys knowing you and desires for you to know Him. You matter to Him.

We could continue indefinitely. We will be exploring and enjoying God's manifold qualities for all eternity. Suffice it to say for now that the Eternal Covenant is a magnificent explosion of revelation. It represents the furthest point in eternity past which God has chosen to reveal to us – the greatest extent to which He draws back the veil of time to allow us to glimpse behind it. As such, the Eternal Covenant is the foundational anchor to our salvation. It is the very first way in which our eternal God stoops to introduce us to Himself. Tremble before Him with fear and joy!

Prayer:

Eternal Father, thank you for promising your Son a people, and for faithfully, lovingly fulfilling that promise. I praise you for mercifully

---

20. Romans 11:33.

21. Mark 14:36.

22. Hebrews 6:17, 18.

23. John 17:5, 6.

24. Psalm 8:4.

including me in that people. As I meditate on your Eternal Covenant, learning more about who you are, move me to worship. I pray this by the enabling Spirit and through the obedient Son with whom you covenanted before the dawn of time, Amen.

Meditation:

Of all of the implications of the Eternal Covenant, which strikes you most? Why?

Day 3
The God Who Knows: Foreknowledge

In 1957, *Popular Mechanics* predicted that by 2020, 'roads and streets will be replaced by a network of pneumatic tubes. Family vehicles will need only a small amount of mobile power, since they will only have to get from the owner's home to a nearby tube.' In 1967, 'The Futurist' predicted that by 2020, our house-cleaning, gardening and chauffeuring would all be done by trained, live-in apes. In 1999, futurist Ray Kurzweil claimed that by 2020, the average American life expectancy would be over one hundred. (It's currently in the seventies.) As Valentine says, in Tom Stoppard's play *Arcadia*, 'We can't even predict the next drip from a dripping tap when it gets irregular. Each drip sets up the conditions for the next. The smallest variation blows prediction apart ... The future is disorder.'[1]

We are wildly delusional about our ability to tell the future. Even the best of human predictions are really only projections based on past and present data. God, on the other hand, knew the future from before the past had even happened.[2] This is because there is no 'past' or 'future' for the God who created time and stands outside of time. For God, everything exists within the ever-present 'now'.[3]

This reality is included in what the Bible calls God's foreknowledge. The two words making up the Greek term for this are *pro* ('before') and *ginosko* ('to know'). It's a term Scripture uses to describe God's

---

1. *Arcadia* by Tom Stoppard (Faber, 1993), p. 51.

2. Ephesians 1:4.

3. John 8:58.

knowledge of His people from eternity past. 'For those whom he foreknew, he also predestined ...'[4]

Yet more than simply factual knowledge of His future people, God's foreknowledge carries the sense of His *loving, saving* knowledge of them. As such, it's one of the links in the so-called Golden Chain of salvation in Romans 8: '*For those whom he foreknew,* he also predestined, ... and those whom he predestined, he also called, and those whom he called he also justified, and those whom he justified he also glorified.'[5]

So foreknowledge is not God's dispassionate awareness of data, but knowledge infused and brimming over with love – a saving love which reached out to us from before the dawn of time. Spurgeon envisions this hauntingly:

> Christ loved you before all worlds; long ere the day star flung his ray across the darkness, before the wing of angel had flapped the unnavigated ether, before aught of creation had struggled from the womb of nothingness, God ... had set his heart upon all his children.[6]

The love inherent in foreknowledge also resonates with Scripture's wider use of the word 'knowledge': it can refer to the intimacy and tenderness of sexual love. 'Now Adam *knew* Eve his wife, and she conceived and bore Cain.'[7] 'Joseph took his wife but *knew* her not until she had given birth.'[8] While clearly asexual, God's foreknowledge of His people is nonetheless a love which is intimate and intense and tender.

The term also implies the merciful, kind, stooping nature of God's love. As the Psalmist exclaims, 'What is man that you are mindful of him, and the son of man that you care for him!'[9] The love within foreknowledge pictures God bending down and caring for miniscule, finite humans – the same humans who, He well knows, will be hating and rejecting Him, to the point of torturing His Son to death. C. S. Lewis imagines this in an arresting passage:

---

4. Romans 8:29.

5. Romans 8:29, 30.

6. Charles Spurgeon, 'A Faithful Friend,' in *Sermons of C. H. Spurgeon* (New York: Sheldon, Blakeman, 1857), p. 13.

7. Genesis 4:1.

8. Matthew 1:24, 25.

9. Psalm 8:4.

He creates the universe, already foreseeing – or should we say 'seeing'? there are no tenses in God – the buzzing crowd of flies around the cross, the flayed back pressed against the uneven stake, the nails driven through the mesial nerves, the repeated insipient suffocation as the body droops, the repeated torture of back and arms as it is time after time, for breath's sake, hitched up ... God is a 'host' who deliberately creates His own parasites; causes us to be that we may exploit and 'take advantage of' Him. Herein is love.[10]

When my wife and I were in the process of adopting, long before we got to see and meet our future sons in the flesh, our social workers started giving us information about them. As we gradually learnt about the tragedies of their backgrounds, their emerging personalities in foster care, their little idiosyncrasies, what made them giggle, their favourite foods, whether they enjoyed baths, what they made of the seaside, and who their teddies were, our hearts welled up with love for them.

I'll never forget the moment when we first received a photo of each of them. (Those photos are on my desk to this day, looking down on me while I write this.) We still wouldn't actually get to be with them for weeks. But our growing knowledge of them as we became intense students of them, was intertwined with passionate, protective, determined love. That's a tiny picture of God's foreknowledge.

Yet we must not misunderstand God's foreknowledge to imply any lessening of His sovereignty over our salvation. Specifically, God does not predestine some to be saved on the basis of having first looked ahead into time and foreseen who would freely choose to believe in Jesus, or even who would be more amenable to the gospel. This would mean that the cause for a believer's salvation lies ultimately in that believer, instead of in God's sovereign grace. As A. W. Pink says, 'False theology makes God's foreknowledge of our believing the cause of his election to salvation; whereas, God's election is the cause and our believing in Christ is the effect.'[11] In the words of the Apostle John, 'We love because he first loved us.'[12]

---

10. C. S. Lewis, *The Four Loves* (Harcourt, 1960), p. 127.

11. Arthur W. Pink, *The Attributes of God* (Baker, 1975), p. 29.

12. 1 John 4:19.

In any case, never in the Bible is God's foreknowledge His knowledge *about* people, such as their future choices. Rather, it is His knowledge *of* people – of people *themselves*: Paul writes 'For *those whom* he foreknew ...'[13] and describes how 'God has not rejected his *people whom* he foreknew.'[14] Scripture's only use of the term towards Jesus resonates with this too: in Peter's words, '*He* was foreknown before the foundation of the world.'[15]

So God's foreknowledge displays His magnificent, all-knowing supremacy over time itself. Yet it also showcases His tender, personal love, while taking nothing from His utter sovereignty.

Here's what all of this means: You can go through today mindful that God knew you before you knew yourself. He planned to be your Father an eternity before you took your first breath. He knows you more accurately and intimately than you will ever know yourself. He loves you more than you can dream. His foreknowledge extends to you overflowing kindness and peace forever, as the Apostle Peter knew: 'Peter, an apostle of Jesus Christ, to those who are elect exiles ... according to the foreknowledge of God the Father ... May grace and peace be multiplied to you.'[16]

Prayer:

All-wise and loving Father, thank you for the grace and peace which is multiplied to me through your foreknowledge of me. Thank you for your infinite, divine knowledge and wisdom, by which you know me better than I will ever know myself. And thank you for your tender, stooping, personal love. Who am I that you should care for me? And yet you do! Help me to take comfort and perspective from these things, no matter what else is going on in my life. In the name of your eternal Son, my older brother in the faith whom you also foreknew, Amen.

Meditation:

How does knowing about God's foreknowledge make you feel? Why?

---

13. Romans 8:29.
14. Romans 11:2.
15. 1 Peter 1:20.
16. 1 Peter 1:1-2.

Day 4
The God Who Chooses: Election

One evening a few years ago, my three-year-old son Nate was riding his scooter around our neighbourhood. He was fearless and of the opinion that breaking and steering were overrated. I jogged alongside him, ever the anxious dad. He was a couple of yards ahead of me on the pavement when I heard the sound of a car rushing towards us, well over the speed limit. Just as it approached, Nate happened to swerve into the road.

Before I knew what I was doing, I had lunged out and grabbed the hood of his jacket. His momentum continued to pull hard against my grip. As the speeding vehicle flew past, inches from his little body, I don't think I've ever held anything as tightly in my life. I'll never forget the horrified look on the driver's face as she realised how close she'd come to ending my son's life. But Nate was not going anywhere. He was secure. I had him.

The doctrine of election can quickly lead to questions, concerns and confusion. These are often valid, and we'll explore some of the bigger ones here. Yet we mustn't forget the primary purpose of the doctrine: despite the hard pull of eternal catastrophe, we are not going anywhere. We are secure. God has us. Our salvation in time has been anchored and locked into eternity past.

Yet as well as this comforting assurance, election is designed to bless us powerfully in further ways, which we'll consider at the end.

Much as election might pose philosophical or moral difficulties for some, Scripture insists on it frequently, throughout the Old Testament as well as through every single New Testament writer: Matthew,[1]

---

1. Matthew 24:22.

Mark,[2] Luke (in both his gospel and the book of Acts),[3] John (in both his gospel and his later writings),[4] Paul,[5] the writer of Hebrews,[6] James,[7] Peter,[8] and Jude.[9] These writers by no means deny the truth of human responsibility and genuine choice, which are scriptural as well. However, our focus here is the divine sovereignty which underpins human responsibility and choice.

So how should we define election?

Election is God's sovereign choice of the individual members of His people for salvation, from before time, on the basis solely of His own will and not of any foreseen merit or faith in them. The Bible's term of predestination carries the same idea.[10]

Here are three commonly raised questions about election:[11]

Does election deny us a genuine choice of belief in Jesus, effectively leaving us as robots? Scripture affirms that we make real, willing, voluntary decisions, including regarding Christ.[12] Our choices are real in that we choose what we genuinely, personally desire to choose.[13] This is not the same as saying that our choices are free.[14] Wonderfully, God's sovereignty extends even to our desires.[15] The idea of absolute freedom from an omnipotent God who sustains all things

---

2. Mark 13:27.

3. Luke 18:7; Acts 13:48.

4. John 15:16, 19; Revelation 17:8.

5. Election features frequently in almost all of Paul's writings. These make up much of the New Testament.

6. Hebrews 2:13 (quoting Isaiah 8:18).

7. James 2:5.

8. 1 Peter 1:1; 2 Peter 1:10.

9. Jude 4.

10. Romans 8:29; Ephesians 1:5,11. The term 'predestination' refers not only to God's foreordination of people (as in election) but also of plans and circumstances. Election is therefore a subset of predestination.

11. Wayne Grudem *Systematic Theology: An Introduction to Biblical Doctrine* (IVP, 1994), pp. 680-684.

12. Acts 2:37-40.

13. Joshua 24:15.

14. Acts 2:37-40.

15. Philippians 2:13.

is oxymoronic. Desiring that would be like a fish desiring to be free from water.[16]

Does election mean, unfairly, that those who reject Christ never had a real chance to receive Him?[17] The Bible is careful to rule out that false assumption. Those who reject Jesus are always culpable, for they are exercising their own genuine, wilful choice. (See above.) Jesus Himself was blunt in asserting this.[18] According to Paul, they are 'without excuse'.[19] What would be *fair* would be for God to consign *all* to what we deserve, just as He consigned *all* angels who sinned to damnation.[20] The fact He saves *any* is a mark of His unmerited mercy. It shouldn't lull us into a sense of entitlement.

Is election based on God looking ahead in time to see who would choose to accept Christ? In some ways this might provide easy answers to the charges of unfairness above. Yet it doesn't quite work. There is a biblical category of God's 'foreknowledge' (see Day 3) but it refers not to facts about individuals or their future choices but to the individuals themselves.[21] In addition, faith is never the reason in Scripture why individuals were elected. The exact opposite is true. The prior election of individuals is the reason that they then have faith.[22] God did not choose us *because* we would have faith but *that* we would have faith.

There is a time for wrestling honestly with these and other undeniably hard truths. However, in the end there is also a need for humility as we stand before Scripture on this subject. God isn't subject to some standard of fairness external to Himself. God Himself *is* the source and arbitrator of fairness. Fairness is, by definition, whatever God chooses to do. At some point we have to admit with Paul, 'But who are you, O man, to answer back to God? Will what is moulded say to its moulder, "Why have you made me like this?" Has the potter

---

16. Acts 17:28.

17. Romans 9:19.

18. John 5:40.

19. Romans 1:20.

20. 2 Peter 2:4.

21. Romans 8:29; 11:2.

22. 1 John 4:19.

no right over the clay ...?'[23] We are the finite creatures, He the infinite Creator. He can do whatever the heaven He likes.

On top of this, we should also remember that our understanding and motives are warped and clouded while His are perfect and unpolluted. His wisdom and love and justice and mercy and grace dwarf ours – they are infinite – and so we must humbly trust His judgement over our own.[24] 'He is the LORD. Let him do what seems good to him.'[25]

So how does God mean to bless us by giving us this doctrine? Here are three examples:

Election grants assurance. As we saw at the start, God has us. His saving grip on us is anchored into eternity past. Absolutely nothing 'in all creation, will be able to separate us from the love of God in Christ Jesus our Lord.'[26] When your own sin or Satan or demons or discouragement or opposition cause you to doubt whether you really will make it all the way to heaven, be heartened. The important thing isn't the strength of your grip on your Father. It is the strength of His grip on you. You are secure.

Election teaches humility. Understanding election will guard us from the dangers of self-destructive pride, which invites God's loving but painful discipline. The only thing we contribute to our salvation is our sin. So this doctrine rightly steers us away from grotesque, farcically inappropriate self-congratulation. Instead it leads us to the humility which honours God and offers us paradoxically *more* assurance, and therefore more confidence and joy.

Election fuels evangelism. If we understand evangelism as trying to persuade people to become Christians, it is indeed pointless in the light of election. But if we rightly understand evangelism as honouring

---

23. Roman 9:20, 21.

24. Romans 11:33-36. Strikingly, these well-known and majestic verses come on the back of three chapters wrestling with election and its implications: 'Oh, the depth of the riches and wisdom and knowledge of God! How unsearchable are his judgments and how inscrutable his ways! "For who has known the mind of the Lord, or who has been his counsellor?" "Or who has given a gift to him that he might be repaid?" For from him and through him and to him are all things. To him be glory forever. Amen.'

25. 1 Samuel 3:18.

26. Romans 8:39.

God by holding out His gospel and calling people to repent and believe, election is the key that unlocks the fruitfulness of evangelism. Our evangelism is God's chosen trigger for revealing the elect.[27] Election means that no one you witness to is necessarily safe: if they were elected, they don't stand a chance against your expressions to them of God's love and mercy, however flawed or faltering your articulation may be. Far from undermining your evangelism, election is precisely what guarantees its efficacy.[28]

As you go into today, let election be a foundation for you of joyful assurance, healthy humility and confident evangelism. Praise the sovereign Father who chooses!

Prayer:

Sovereign God, I thank you for the beautiful truth of election. Allow me to understand this doctrine accurately, the way you present it to me in your Word. Grant me to humble myself before you where I find it difficult. Help me to receive through it comfort and assurance, humility, motivation for evangelism, and a greater vision of your majesty. In the name of One in whom I am chosen, Amen.

Meditation:

How does the truth of election instinctively make you feel? Why?

---

27. Acts 13:48.

28. Acts 18:9-11; 2 Timothy 2:10.

Act II
Life Begins

Day 5
The God Who Arranges: Providence

Following His agreement to redeem you (Day 2), His loving foreknowledge of you (Day 3), and His sovereign election of you (Day 4), God arranged all the details of your future life on earth, from the millisecond of your conception to your final heartbeat. He arranged that you would be reading this sentence right now.

And more than simply controlling everything perfectly, He also controls everything *lovingly*, for the good of His people. This is known as His providence. Romans 8:28 describes it like this: 'And we know that for those who love God, *all things* work together for good, for those who are called according to his purpose.'

The extent of God's providence in 'all things' is beyond mind-boggling. Take for example a hair. A typical human hair is about a hundred thousand atoms in width. Pluck one right now and contemplate that for a moment. A hundred thousand. In *width*.

Each one of those hundred thousand atoms has at its centre a nucleus consisting of neutrons and protons. Each nucleus is made up of further sub-particles. And around each nucleus spins electrons. Each electron orbits its nucleus at around 2,200km per second. Pause for a second and try to visualise something travelling at 2,200km per second.

Done that? Because it's practically standing still compared to the rate at which an atom's nucleus can rotate: about a hundred billion, billion revolutions per second.

Here's the point: God created each atom in the universe – that's a fair few if you remember the width of a human hair – and set them in motion, and controls each one precisely. You might say He is quite good at spinning plates (and nuclei). 'He *upholds the universe by the word of his power.*'[1] Yet even these examples are the tiniest tip of the iceberg. As the book of Job marvels at, we know only 'the outskirts of his ways, and how small a whisper do we hear of him! But the thunder of his power who can understand?'[2]

The biblical writers may not have known about atomic nuclei or electrons, but they did observe the same truth in their own world: 'The lot is cast into the lap, but its every decision is from the Lord.'[3]

While God ensures that all things work together for our good, this doesn't of course mean that all things that happen to us *are* good. Perhaps horrendous evil has been committed against you. If so, it *was* evil. In fact, God, being perfect, mourns and hates it even more than you. One day He will judge it with righteous fury. But providence says that in the meantime He unfailingly brings good *out* of evil.[4] Like a judo fighter expertly using the momentum of an opponent's strike for his own advantage, He uses it.

But the judo picture shouldn't be pushed too far to imply that God is simply quick and clever at reacting to evil. His providence is not merely skilful improvising, or rolling with the punches of sin and Satan. *Pronoia*, the Greek word from which we get 'providence', means '*fore*thought'. He knows the end from the beginning.[5] Not one sparrow falls to the ground without His prior, sovereign consent.[6]

At the same time, while all things including evil happen inside God's consent, this doesn't mean He is the author of evil, or that He endorses it or encourages people to commit it. Scripture is clear that He unfailingly hates evil, and is always innocent of it.[7] Providence is the loving operation of a wholly good God.[8]

---

1. Hebrews 1:3.

2. Job 26:14.

3. Proverbs 16:33.

4. Genesis 50:20.

5. Isaiah 46:10.

6. Matthew 10:29.

7. James 1:13; 1 John 1:5.

8. The paradox of these two truths – that nothing happens outside of God's predestination and consent, yet also that He is completely innocent of all evil – is

True story: recently, with little warning to my five-year-old, I drove him to a nearby building and led him into a small room. The sight of it filled him with sudden fear because of what he had experienced there once before. When we got inside, I shut the door behind us, overpowered his frantic struggles, pinned his arms to his sides, and enabled another adult to hurt him. This adult stabbed him, and the stab was sudden and deep. There was blood. He wept inconsolably.

That's dark and awful isn't it? Maybe it sounds like a metaphor for something you're enduring in this season of your own life. It's a description of Teddy's chickenpox inoculation, which will safeguard him from great, potentially fatal suffering for the rest of his life. The building was a medical centre and the other adult was a sweet-natured nurse who had a soft spot for Teddy. As well as the inoculation, she gave him a cartoon plaster before I whisked him away for prolonged huggles, a browse in a toy shop, and a promised ice cream. All is not as it may seem in our sufferings.

Even when I can see no possible way in which events could be for my good, I can trust my heavenly Father. Holocaust survivor Corrie Ten Boom said, 'When a train goes through a tunnel and it gets dark, you don't throw away the ticket and jump off. You sit still and trust the engineer.' The Apostle Paul wrote, 'How unsearchable are his judgements and how inscrutable his ways!'[9]

The cross is the ultimate example of good from evil – seemingly hopeless, irredeemable, infinitely heinous evil. There humanity tortured to death its Creator's beloved, innocent, precious Son. Yet in the book of Acts, believers can praise God for the cross as something that '... your hand and your plan had predestined to take place.'[10] From the worst evil in the history of the world, God brought about the greatest good: the eternal salvation of millions upon millions, to His everlasting glory. And if the Lord is able providentially to bring that kind of good out of that kind of evil, how much more can you trust Him in even the seemingly hopeless tragedies of your own life!

---

a different and deeper discussion. Yet we can confidently hold to both, as Scripture does. For an in-depth biblical exploration of this, see *The Providence of God* by Paul Helm (IVP, 1993).

9. Romans 11:33.

10. Act 4:28.

I like to say to my sons at the start of a day, 'I wonder what God has in store for us today!' Whatever He has in store for you for the rest of today – and all of your remaining days on earth – you have at your disposal unshakeable peace and deep-down contentment. Human nature is such that even as believers, sadly, we won't always choose it. But it is always available.

Providence also means we have a licence to live for Jesus joyfully and fearlessly, knowing that we cannot lose. Providence is the safety net under the tightrope. It's the safety harness as we climb the cliff. Providence means heading into battle for the Kingdom each day cheerfully, audaciously, without trepidation or inhibition. As John Newton wrote to a friend towards the end of his life, 'All shall work together for good: everything is needful that He sends; nothing can be needful that He withholds.'[11]

Prayer:

Sovereign God, thank you for providence. Thank you that for me your child, all things work together for good. Grant me the peace and joy that come from accepting this truth. Help me to trust you for it when I can't see it. And help me to live for you joyfully and fearlessly, knowing that all things are in your hands. In the name of Jesus who is head over all, Amen.

Meditation:

What do you think can sometimes cause Christians to deny to themselves (emotionally even if not intellectually) the reality of God's providence?

---

11. *The Works of John Newton,* Ed. Richard Cecil (London: Hamilton, Adams & Co., 1824), 2:147.

Day 6
The God Who Creates:
Conception and Physical Life

Having ordained in His providence precisely when, where and to whom you would be born, your Creator set about the miracle of assembling you physically.

> *For you formed my inward parts;*
> *   you knitted me together in my mother's womb.*
> *I praise you, for I am fearfully and wonderfully made.*
> *Wonderful are your works;*
> *   my soul knows it very well.*
> *My frame was not hidden from you,*
> *when I was being made in secret,*
> *   intricately woven in the depths of the earth.*
> *Your eyes saw my unformed substance;*
> *in your book were written, every one of them,*
> *   the days that were formed for me,*
> *   when as yet there was none of them.[1]*

In what sense have you been 'fearfully and wonderfully made'?

For starters, your conception began with hundreds of millions of sperms racing for an egg. That egg had sophisticated receptors on its surface to ensure that only one sperm would ever gain entry to fertilise it. And so you began. (Anyone who's ever told you that you are one in a million is selling you woefully short. You are one in several hundred million.)

---

1. Psalm 139:13-16.

Shortly after this, you took the form of a single cell measuring one tenth of a millimetre, yet containing one million millimetres' length of DNA. Within a week you were signalling to your mother that she was pregnant by releasing your own hormone. You did this to get her to produce more progesterone for her uterus lining so that you might safely implant there. (Well done!)

A fortnight later, your heart (by now the size of a pinhead) was beating and your brain was dividing into three distinct sections. In another three weeks, your body was starting to make reflexive movements.

Fast-forward to twenty weeks and you had your adult taste buds. You were swimming, kicking, turning and even doing somersaults. You were dreaming, indicated by your Rapid Eye Movement sleep, your vocal cords worked, and you recognised your mother's voice.

We could go on recounting this slow-motion, beyond-spectacular miracle. Even the things mentioned here barely scratch the surface. The point is that Psalm 139 isn't wrong. You were fearfully and wonderfully made. You were intricately woven. Behold the Great Weaver's imagination, wisdom, skill and tender care! And as it all unfolded, you were being lovingly gazed upon. 'My frame was not hidden from you when I was being made in secret ... Your eyes saw my unformed substance.'[2] During your birth and all that led up to it, your truest Father was looking down with more joy and love than all the dads at all the births of all their children since the world began. Yet the simplest and greatest way in which you are fearfully and wonderfully made is this: you are His image-bearer.[3] You reflect Him. You are a chip off the divine block. Quite apart from your workmanship and intricacy, your spirituality, morality, creativity, intellectuality and immortality started pumping echoes of your magnificent Maker out into the universe. And they will be doing so forever. Praise Him!

What else can we take from the extraordinary miracle of your arrival into world? Here are some further things:[4]

---

2. Psalm 139:15, 16.

3. Genesis 1:26.

4. I am grateful to Dr Tyler Scarlett for these points in his blog post 'A theology of childbirth.' See http://www.forestbaptistchurch.org/621-2/# Accessed November 2021.

Your birth points to God's goodness in this world. Every kind of person experiences God's universal kindness through the gift of little ones: Christians on fire for the Lord, back-sliders, atheists, those of other religions, upstanding citizens, those on the margins of society, the wealthy, the homeless, the successful, and those who've made a mess of their lives. The miraculous gift of children comes lovingly from the same God who 'makes his sun rise on the evil and on the good, and sends rain on the just and on the unjust'.[5] What a kind and generous God we have!

Your birth points to the fallenness of this world. Anthony Doerr indicates this reality with a telling description in his novel *All The Light We Cannot See*:

> We begin as a microscopic electrical swarm. The lungs, the brain the heart. Forty weeks later, six trillion cells get crushed in the vice of our mother's birth canal and we howl. Then the world starts in on us.[6]

In addition to every baby, every mother undergoing the agony of childbirth has also been experiencing the curse of the Fall – the same curse which first came upon Eve: 'I will surely multiply your pain in childbearing; in pain you shall bring forth children.'[7] Just as Adam's curse meant pain in his kind of labour, so Eve's curse also meant pain (the same word in Hebrew) in hers.[8]

These curses were the result of human sin. We love to try to conceal and deny our sin, just as Adam and Eve did, hiding that day in the garden.[9] Childbirth is one of the painful reminders by which God denies us that self-destructive luxury. The pain of childbirth is a sobering reminder from an honest and realistic God about the seriousness of sin.

Your birth points to the Saviour of this world. Throughout Scripture, God's classic pattern is to infuse judgement with grace. Along with the curses of the Fall came a promise. One day, God assured our first parents, there would come the birth of the Serpent-

---

5. Matthew 5:45.

6. Anthony Doerr, *All the Light We Cannot See* (Scribner, 2014), p. 468.

7. Genesis 3:16.

8. Genesis 3:17.

9. Genesis 3:8.

Crusher, the Satan-defeater, the Saviour.[10] The Old Testament is the story of God's people waiting and hoping, century after century, for that birth. Then the great day finally arrived. Upon discovering her pregnancy, Mary burst out in a magnificent paeon of praise. Upon being presented with the neonatal Jesus, Simeon did likewise.[11] The Eternal Word had become flesh.[12]

Let the thought of your own nine-month journey from conception to birth point you to the One who travelled that same route into this world to rescue you. For you, He allowed his six trillion cells also to be crushed in the vice of his mother's birth canal. He too howled. He too had the world start in on Him.

Your birth points to the means of salvation in this world:

> Jesus answered him, 'Truly, truly I say to you, unless one is born again, he cannot see the kingdom of God.' Nicodemus said to him, 'How can a man be born when he is old? Can he enter a second time into his mother's womb and be born?' Jesus answered, 'Truly, truly, I say to you, unless one is born of water and the Spirit, he cannot enter the kingdom of God.'[13]

Physical birth into this world is God's picture for the spiritual birth by which we enter His kingdom. As someone has said, 'If you are born once, you will die twice. But if you are born twice, you will only die once.' Let your birth remind you of the Christ whose birth into this world paved the way for your rebirth into the glorious world to come.

Prayer:

Creator God, thank you that my physical existence as one who is fearfully and wonderfully made points to your wisdom and love. I praise you for your imagination and power on display in my conception and birth. Would these things enlarge my view of you and increase my worship of you. Would the painful nature of my birth be a sobering reminder of the truth about this fallen

10. Genesis 3:15.
11. Luke 1:46-55; Luke 2:28-32.
12. John 1:14.
13. John 3:3-5.

world. But would it also point me to your goodness, to your Son and to your salvation. In the name of Jesus of Nazareth who took on flesh, Amen.

Meditation:

Of the implications of your conception and birth mentioned here, which strikes you the most? Why?

Day 7
The God Who Proclaims:
External Call

I was privileged as a boy to have devoted Christ-followers as parents. Growing up, I heard the gospel thousands of times. Yet day after day, for year after year, the good news of Jesus bounced off this proud, complacent, self-righteous, Bible-knowing child.

Then one evening when I was twelve, on a last-minute whim, I went along to hear a Christian talk. I went partly for the chocolates afterwards and partly to hang out with others I knew would be there. The talk was simply a short explanation of the cross. As a piece of rhetoric, it was unremarkable. The content was nothing I hadn't heard many times already, and even assented to. Yet that evening, I was suddenly, deeply convicted as never before, of the message of Christ crucified. Later that night, I knelt by my bed, shaken, and truly repented and believed for the very first time.

So what was going on during those thousands of previous times the message of the gospel had bounced off me? The answer is God's external call, otherwise known as His gospel call or His general call. This is God's call to any and all, elect and non-elect, to repent and believe. 'He commands all people everywhere to repent.'[1]

Unlike God's internal call which comes from the Father[2] and is irresistible,[3] God's external call comes from the witness of believers and doesn't in itself have power to convert. Jesus distinguishes between the two calls in His parable of the wedding feast in Matthew 22, which

---

1. Acts 17:30.
2. Romans 8:29; 1 Corinthians 1:9.
3. Romans 8:30.

finishes with these words: 'For many are called [external call] but few are chosen [internal call]'.[4] The same distinction is described by Paul:

> We preach Christ crucified [external call], a stumbling block to Jews and folly to Gentiles, but to those who are called [internal call], both Jews and Greeks, Christ the power of God and the wisdom of God.[5]

This raises a question. If the external call – our own witnessing – doesn't have the power to convert, if in Jesus' words it is calling people who haven't been chosen, if in Paul's words it is putting stumbling blocks and folly before its hearers, what's the point? Why bother with evangelism if only the Father's internal call can achieve anything?

The answer is that the point of evangelism isn't to persuade people to become Christians! Evangelism is the emitting of the fragrance of life to those who are being saved but also the emitting of death to those who aren't.[6] The point of evangelism, along with the point of everything else in the universe, is to glorify God. All of creation, in Calvin's helpful picture, amounts to a 'platform' – a 'dazzling theatre' – for God's glory.[7] Any faithful presentation of the good news of Jesus, even before we consider hearers' responses, glorifies God *by definition*. This is because it sets on display His love, grace, mercy, holiness, justice and wisdom. And that display is witnessed, which amounts to God's glory. Humans witness the display, even if just the two in the conversation, and even if the unbeliever is denying what is in view. Angels and demons may well witness the display. Most importantly of all, the members of the Trinity witness the display.

In addition, there is also a second, more terrible way in which God is glorified when we evangelise. To explain this, we need to back up a touch: The external call is powerless to convert not because there is anything wrong with it but because its hearers are spiritually helpless to respond. However, helplessness doesn't always imply innocence.

Picture two drivers in two separate car crashes. Neither has a chance to steer accurately. Both plough into a pedestrian with tragic

---

4. Matthew 22:14.

5. 1 Corinthians 1:23, 24.

6. 2 Corinthians 2:15, 16.

7. John Calvin, *The Institutes of the Christian Religion*, ed. John T. McNeill, trans. Ford L. Battles, 2 vols. (Louisville, KY: Westminster John Knox, 1960), 1.14.20; 1.5.8; 6.2.1.

consequences. The first driver was helpless because of a fault in the car's steering mechanism, for which he wasn't responsible. The second driver was helpless because of the six beers he chugged before climbing into the car. We are the second driver. Our helplessness in the face of God's external call is morally culpable. Our helplessness is because of our sin.[8]

Here, therefore, is how God is glorified by the helpless yet still culpable non-response of wicked rebels: their continued disobedience towards His external call increasingly heaps up their guilt and with it, their eternal condemnation.[9] And in that awful, tragic eternity to come, the glory of God's holiness, purity, righteousness, justice, power and intolerance of evil will blaze brightly forever.[10] This is why, at the destruction of God's enemies at the end of time, an angel will cry, 'Fear God *and give him glory* because the hour of his judgement has come'.[11]

To be clear, the Lord takes 'no pleasure in the death of the wicked'.[12] He experiences intense grief over the eternal loss of rebels.[13] In one sense, He urgently 'desires all people to be saved.'[14] At one level of His will,[15] He doesn't 'wish that any should perish.'[16] Yet at the same time, on another level, it is part of His plan: 'The Lord has made everything

---

8. Ephesians 2:1-3.

9. Romans 2:5.

10. Psalm 58:10, 11; Romans 9:17, 21, 22; Revelation 19:1-5.

11. Revelation 14:7.

12. Ezekiel 33:11.

13. Luke 19:41-44.

14. 1 Timothy 2:4.

15. Scripture indicates that there are two distinct wills in God: His sovereign will and His moral will, otherwise known as His secret will and His revealed will. The former refers to everything God has sovereignly ordained to happen, in the minutest detail, from before the creation of the world. He typically keeps these things hidden and secret from us until they occur. The latter refers to the things God has openly revealed He loves and hates, the things which *in principle* He commands or forbids. God's plan to receive glory from defeated rebels occurs on the level of His sovereign will. God's simultaneous desire that none should perish occurs on the level of His moral will. This distinction may seem strange at first, but the same exists within humans: as a parent, my sovereign will may be at times to cause the pain of discipline to my son – even while my moral will continues to be that he should not experience pain. This distinction in the wills of God also makes sense of scenarios such as God's prohibition and hatred of murder, yet simultaneous plan for the death of his Son at the hands of the Jews and the Romans.

16. 2 Peter 3:9.

for its purpose, even the wicked for the day of trouble.'[17] The manifest defeat of defiant opponents (such as ourselves, but for His grace) is within His purpose and brings Him glory:

> For the Scripture says to Pharaoh [who God condemned], 'For this very purpose I have raised you up, *that I might show my power in you, and that my name might be proclaimed in all the earth.'*... What if God, *desiring to show his wrath and to make known his power,* has endured with much patience vessels of wrath prepared for destruction ...?[18]

If our hearts are healthy and not sadistic, we will long for people to repent and believe, for the Father to join His internal call to our external call. This is God's heart. It was also Paul's. At the start of the section of Romans in which Paul penned the hard-to-hear verses above, Paul writes of his feelings towards the lost, 'I have great sorrow and unceasing anguish in my heart.'[19] Ultimately however, the results column of our evangelism is the Lord's. Our role in evangelism is to put the gospel before the lost around us with all the love and clarity we can muster. Doing this redounds to God's glory, as does even humanity's response of disobedience and rejection.

As well as God's glory, here are some further purposes behind God's external call:

Our privilege. Evangelism is not something we *have* to do, as much as something we *get* to do. Peter describes believers as 'a chosen race, a royal priesthood, a holy nation ... that you may proclaim the excellencies of him who called you out of darkness into his marvellous light'.[20] What a privilege to represent the Lord Jesus to those around us as His appointed ambassadors![21]

Our growth. Proclaiming God's external call is not easy but that is partly the point. It affords believers amazing personal growth opportunities. Evangelism is the Christian's training ground for growth in love, courage, compassion, faithfulness, and theological accuracy.[22]

---

17. Proverbs 16:4.
18. Romans 9:17, 22.
19. Romans 9:2.
20. 1 Peter 2:9.
21. 2 Corinthians 5:20.
22. 2 Peter 1:5-7.

Our humanhood. When God's external call to us is joined by His internal call, our (divinely enabled) response to the external call means we have been saved not as robot-like automatons but as humans with genuine agency and responsibility. Our God-glorifying humanhood is in evidence.

Our encouragement. Your act of witnessing, regardless of the consequences, in itself is a glorious accomplishment of God's mission for you on earth. You've been tasked with sounding the call, not raising the dead. That's God's job. So no matter how faltering or apparently ineffective your witnessing might seem at times, feel a right sense of victory as you engage in it. Feel justified fulfilment. Feel your Father's pleasure in you as He looks down on your faithful pursuit of your mission.

Prayer:

God of the whole earth, I praise you for the broadcast of your truth through the mouths of your people. Thank you for glorifying yourself through the display of the message of Christ before countless millions. Help me to be encouraged, faithful, expectant and bold as I embrace the privilege and undergo the training of putting out that external call. In the name of the Son who you gave because of your love for the whole world, Amen.

Meditation:

Of the purposes behind God's external call, which do you think you need to hear most? Why?

Day 8
The God Who Summons:
Internal Call

One of the highlights of my day is taking our golden retriever Charlie to a nearby nature reserve for an hour each evening. Sometimes to his delight we're joined by some of his many canine buddies and their owners. One evening, it was time for Charlie and I to leave the group and start heading home, and I began walking away. Some of the other owners walking with me saw that Charlie wasn't coming and started calling his name. However, their friendly shouts to him didn't even compete with the delights of sniffing Ranger's bottom or trying to get Fido to chase him. He never even looked up.

Then I pulled out my dog whistle. From a couple of hundred yards away I gave three short blasts at thirty-five kilohertz, outside the range of human hearing. His head snapped round. Before he knew what he was doing, he started haring towards me, tongue out, ears back, all else forgotten. He was overtaken with a joyful, all-consuming focus on his master. (That's my version of events anyway and I'm sticking to it.)

As we saw yesterday, God's external call comes through the gospel witness of believers and doesn't itself have the power to summon people to repentance and faith. However, for the elect, there comes a time when God adds to that external call His internal call. Having been deaf to believers' previous evangelistic entreaties, our hearts are pierced and awakened by a sovereign summons we can't help recognising. This call is indiscernible to human perception but at the sound of it we find ourselves inexorably drawn to our true and loving master.

Here, then, are some of the features of God's internal call:

It is specifically from the Father.[1] Otherwise known as His effective call or definite call, this call is irreversible and unalterable. 'For the gifts and the calling of God are irrevocable.'[2] When our Father calls, we are His for keeps. The orphans are never summoned from hopelessness to eternal joy and freedom only for the message not to get through.

It is irresistible. When He calls, we come. Neither Satan, nor sin, nor anything else in all creation can defeat the efficacy of our master's sovereign summons.[3] Notice the link of the internal call in the unbreakable chain of salvation: 'And those whom he predestined *he also called, and those whom he called* he also justified, and those whom he justified he also glorified.'[4]

It is personal. God doesn't shout out a number, consult a list and then usher the next believer past without bothering to look up. He knows who He calls and calls who He knows. Each son or daughter of His matters to Him as His precious handiwork, in His image, with whom He has planned to spend eternity. 'Thus says the Lord, he who created you O Jacob, he who formed you O Israel: "Fear not, for I have redeemed you; I have called you *by name*, you are mine."'[5] Jesus Himself said as much: 'The sheep hear his voice, and he calls his own sheep *by name* and leads them out.'[6]

It is unique in its effectiveness. God's internal call is not only paternal, irrevocable, irresistible and personal. It is also the only way we can be reached. It is the one safe lane through the minefield of our wrath-deserving, sin-soaked spiritual helplessness. 'No one can come to me' taught Jesus, 'unless the Father who sent me draws him.'[7]

It is typically placed by God alongside His external call via a believer.[8] John Wesley's account of his own conversion is a famous example. This is from his diary entry for the twenty-fourth of May, 1738:

---

1. 1 Corinthians 1:9. See also Romans 8:28.
2. Romans 11:29.
3. Romans 8:38, 39.
4. Romans 8:30.
5. Isaiah 43:1.
6. John 10:3.
7. John 6:44.
8. Romans 10:14.

> In the evening I went very unwillingly to a society in Aldersgate Street, where one was reading Luther's preface to the Epistle to the Romans. About a quarter before nine, while he was describing the change which God works in the heart through faith in Christ, I felt my heart strangely warmed. I felt I did trust in Christ, Christ alone, for salvation; and an assurance was given me that He had taken away my sins, even mine, and saved me from … sin and death.[9]

However, the Father is not constrained to make external and internal calls simultaneous. Consider the remarkable testimony of Luke Short. A farmer in New England, he was sitting in his fields one day aged a 103, reflecting on his long life. He recalled a sermon he had listened to eighty-five years earlier as a boy in Dartmouth, before sailing for America. As he meditated on the truths he had heard as a teenager, his heart was opened and he gave his life to Christ. His Father had finally called him home.

It is also worth drinking in the beautiful range of Scripture's descriptions of that *to which* God has called us. This includes:

- The ability to do the impossible and come to Jesus[10]
- Ownership by Christ[11]
- Fellowship with God's Son[12]
- God's kingdom and glory[13]
- Marvellous light[14]
- Sainthood[15]
- Glory[16]
- Peace[17]
- Freedom[18]

---

9. John Wesley, *The Journal of John Wesley* (London: C. H. Kelly, 1903).
10. John 6:44.
11. Romans 1:6.
12. 1 Corinthians 1:9.
13. 1 Thessalonians 2:12.
14. 1 Peter 2:9.
15. Romans 1:7.
16. Romans 8:30.
17. 1 Corinthians 7:15.
18. Galatians 5:13.

- Hope[19]
- Holiness[20]
- Endurance[21]
- Eternal life[22]

Each of these describe different aspects of the same reality: salvation. God's call is like a priceless diamond rotating in a showcase under the light of Scripture which shows off its multi-faceted beauty. As Paul bursts out, having examined God's salvation in depth, 'Oh the depth of the riches and wisdom and knowledge of God! ... To Him be glory forever!'[23] Praise Him!

As well as worship and thankfulness, what else can we take from this doctrine? Here are three further things:

Humility. I cannot steal glory from God for my own positive response to the evangelism of others. Similarly, I cannot steal glory from God for the responses of others to *my* evangelism. It is God's internal call alone that raises the spiritually dead. '[Paul] related one by one the things that God had done among the Gentiles through his ministry. And when they heard it, they glorified God.'[24]

Prayerfulness. The truth of God's inward call means that evangelism which isn't saturated in prayer may well be a waste of time. Certainly, prayer-less evangelism isn't honouring to the Lord. Our skill is not the decisive factor in our witnessing. Neither is our passion or our courage or our charisma or even our faithfulness. It is our Father. Talking to others about God is nothing without talking to God about others. Paul knew this when he wrote about his lost kinsmen, 'My heart's desire and prayer to God for them is that they may be saved.'[25]

Assurance. God's internal call to you was your loving Father's irrevocable, irresistible, sovereign summons. It was His unbreak-

---

19. Ephesians 1:18.
20. 1 Thessalonians 4:7.
21. 1 Peter 3:9.
22. 1 Timothy 6:12.
23. Romans 11:33, 36.
24. Acts 21:19, 20.
25. Romans 10:1.

able, unassailable, inexorable lifeline to you. It was your Daddy's summoning cry of love to wake the dead.

Prayer:

Dear Father, thank you for calling me. Thank you for the power *of your call to wake the dead. Thank you for the* love *of your call to bestow everlasting life. In your kindness, warm my heart to praise you all the more joyfully for your merciful summons. In the name of the Christ to whom you called me, Amen.*

Meditation:

Of the Bible's range of descriptions above of what God has called you to, which strikes you the most right now? Why?

Day 9

The God Who Enlivens: Regeneration

As we saw yesterday, the internal call is God's summoning cry of love to wake the dead. Regeneration is the actual waking, the spiritual resurrection, which results from that call. If the internal call is Jesus crying into Lazarus' tomb with a loud voice, 'Come out!',[1] then regeneration is the spiritual equivalent of the enzymes and molecules of the corpse reconstituting, the electrical impulses returning to his brain, his heart restarting, and Lazarus sitting up. If you are reading these words as a believer, that is what you have experienced. Let's take a closer look at some key characteristics of God's astounding miracle of regeneration. Here are four of them:

Regeneration is a gift of life to the dead. 'And you were dead in the trespasses and sins in which you once walked … But God, being rich in mercy, because of the great love with which he loved us, even when we were dead in our trespasses, made us alive together with Christ.'[2]

It wasn't that you were spiritually unconscious and needed help coming around, or confused and needed educating, or cynical and needed persuading. In terms of your ability to relate to God, you were stone cold dead. Spiritually, your inert soul had long since putrefied. Then the Lord of life performed a miracle upon you.

---

1. John 11:43.
2. Ephesians 2:1, 2, 4, 5.

In fact, it was a miracle up there with the creation of the universe: 'For God, who said, "Let light shine out of darkness," has shone in our hearts to give the light of the knowledge of the glory of God in the face of Jesus Christ.'[3] It was a miracle up there with the resurrection of Jesus: in working it, God used 'the immeasurable greatness of his power toward us who believe, according to the working of his great might that he worked in Christ when he raised him from the dead.'[4] Don't underestimate what God did in you, for you to be reading this as His living child.

Regeneration is a gift entirely from God. Being dead, we had no role in the miracle of life performed upon us. As John says, he 'gave the right to become children of God [to those] who were born, *not of blood nor of the will of the flesh nor of the will of man*, but of God.'[5]

We chose to be regenerated spiritually as much as we chose to exist physically. We can take as much credit for our regeneration as a new-born baby can take for its birth. This is partly in view in the Bible's repeated analogy of physical birth. 'Unless one is born again, he cannot see the Kingdom of God.'[6]

So our regeneration was not synergistic, that is, arising through the combination of our contribution and God's contribution. Our regeneration was monergistic – solely and exclusively of God. We mustn't be like someone a friend of mine knew – let's call him Phil. Phil once turned up at a birthday party without a gift, realised he should have brought one, and quickly scribbled on the label of the gift someone else had brought '... and from Phil'. Regeneration isn't a gift partly from God and partly from us to ourselves. We mustn't be glory thieves.

Regeneration is a gift from the Father and the Spirit. As we saw on Day 2, members of the Trinity do not act independently of each other. Having said that, different actions are often led by different

---

3. 2 Corinthians 4:6.

4. Ephesians 1:19, 20.

5. John 1:12, 13.

6. John 3:3. See also 1 Peter 1:3, and James 1:18 which uses language in the Greek for describing physical birth ('brought us forth').

persons. In the case of regeneration, the Bible presents the Father as the source. Paul writes that 'God made [you] alive together with him [Christ]';[7] Peter describes how 'the God and Father of our Lord Jesus Christ … has caused us to be born again to a living hope'.[8] James similarly identifies regeneration as coming from 'the Father of lights'.[9]

At the same time, Jesus is clear to Nicodemus in John's gospel that regeneration comes by the Holy Spirit: 'Unless one is born of water and the Spirit, he cannot enter the kingdom of God.'[10] Nicodemus' question in John 3 isn't about the cause or source of regeneration but its application to the believer, hence Jesus citing the Spirit rather than the Father. Throughout Scripture, the Spirit's role is often to enact and apply the work of the other persons of the Trinity. Regeneration comes from the Father, by the Spirit.

Know that the unified Trinity was operating in your spiritual resurrection. Think of the Father and the Spirit rejoicing together as they worked alongside each other to raise you for the Son. What a wonderful triune God we have!

Regeneration is a gift that produces repentance and faith – not the other way around. R. C. Sproul describes this helpfully: 'It is not as if dead people have faith, and because of their faith God agrees to regenerate them. Rather, it is because God has regenerated us and given us new life that we have faith.'[11] Logically, if we were spiritually dead, then regeneration – being brought to life – must be the cause rather than the effect of any spiritual activity on our part. Yet this isn't only logical. It's biblical:

> According to James, it was not because of our own repentance and faith that He gave us new birth, but 'of his own will'.[12]

> According to Peter, it was not because of any action of ours that He caused us to be born again, but 'according to his great mercy'.[13]

---

7. Colossians 2:13.

8. 1 Peter 1:3.

9. James 1:17.

10. John 3:5.

11. R. C. Sproul, *Tabletalk*, 1989.

12. James 1:18.

13. 1 Peter 1:3.

According to John, it is not that everyone who has been born of God had already believed, but the opposite: 'everyone who believes ... has been born of God.'[14]

According to Paul, the first thing we experience of salvation, as those who are blind, is when God shines 'in our hearts to give the light of the knowledge of the glory of God in the face of Jesus Christ'.[15]

According to Luke, it is not that Lydia pays attention to Paul's gospel and so the Lord opens her heart, but the opposite: 'The Lord opened her heart to pay attention to what was said by Paul.'[16]

Praise the God of life for doing everything, giving everything, causing everything needed for our salvation. 'For from him and through him and to him are all things. To him be glory forever. Amen.'[17]

Prayer:

Father, thank you that I am able to pray to you right now as your child because you raised me to spiritual life. Thank you for reaching into my utter helplessness, and with the Spirit, for the Son, performing upon me the astounding miracle of spiritual resurrection. Thank you for all that comes from this gift, beginning with my repentance and faith. I praise you for the Spirit by whom you raised me, in the name of the Son for whom you raised me, Amen.

Meditation:

In the light of this doctrine of regeneration, how would you describe God?

---

14. 1 John 5:1.

15. 2 Corinthians 4:6.

16. Acts 16:14.

17. Romans 11:36.

Day 10

The God Who Converts:
Repentance and Faith

Imagine a wooden cross, the kind on which Jesus was crucified, but large enough to contain an open doorway. You can see carved over that doorway words of Jesus: 'Come to me all you who are weary and burdened and I will give you rest.'[1] This is God's external call (Day 7). You step through the doorway. Looking back, you then see another inscription over the door, on the side where you now stand. It quotes words from Ephesians: 'Chosen before the foundation of the world.'[2] This is God's election (Day 4), most helpfully seen in hindsight, as a wonderful guarantee of your eternal security. Here is how your conversion fits into this analogy: It is your action of stepping through the doorway. It is your repentance and faith. It is your own first activity in your salvation journey. Let's take a closer look by considering the following five questions:

1. What are repentance and faith?

'Repent and believe in the gospel!' proclaims Jesus at the start of His ministry in Mark's gospel.[3] What does Jesus mean? 'Gospel' literally means 'good news'. It is the best news in the world that although we are sinful and deserve eternal judgement, God sent His Son to die to pay for our sin, so that all who trust in His sacrifice may be forgiven and have eternal life.[4] To 'repent' means to turn *from* our sin – to

---

1. Matthew 11:28 (NIV).
2. Ephesians 1:4.
3. Mark 1:15.
4. John 3:16.

acknowledge it as the God-dishonouring, self-destructive wickedness which it is, to own our guilt for it, to beg God's forgiveness for it, and to declare war on it. Alongside the repentance of turning *from* is the faith of turning *to*. To 'believe' means to turn *to* Jesus – to come to Him with faith in His death to deal for our sin. It means to entrust ourselves and our sin and our eternity to our new, true Master.

Far from being cliched jargon, or tick-boxes to be casual with, repentance and faith are the two doorposts of the entrance to glory. They are the two borders of the path to eternal life. Treasure them.

2. What are repentance and faith not?

Faith is more than simply believing certain facts to be true. 'Show me your faith apart from your works, and I will show you my faith by my works. You believe that God is one; you do well. Even the demons believe – and shudder!'[5] Saving faith isn't merely intellectual assent. Ask Satan and his angels. True faith is a God-honouring dependence on Christ for salvation.

As well as faith being more than just knowledge, so repentance is more than just sorrow. 'Godly grief produces a repentance that leads to salvation without regret, whereas worldly grief produces death.'[6] Repentance isn't the grief of self-pity, or the grief of sin's practical consequences, or even grief at personal failure. Those are examples of worldly grief. Repentance is 'godly grief' – grief which feels the pain of dishonouring God, which acknowledges guilt before God, and which longs for the forgiveness of God. Puritan Thomas Brooks called repentance 'the vomit of the soul'. It is the consistent, committed, determined rejection of that which is catastrophically toxic.

Guard the distinction in your heart between mere knowledge and a whole-hearted leaning on Jesus for salvation, and between mere regret and a sorrowful thrusting away of all sin. Therein lies your salvation.

3. How do repentance and faith relate to each other?

Repentance and faith are different sides of the same coin. They describe perspectives on the same single act of turning. This is why they are paired in Scripture. Paul testifies 'of repentance toward God and of

---

5. James 2:18, 19.

6. 2 Corinthians 7:10.

faith in our Lord Jesus Christ'.[7] The writer to the Hebrews speaks of 'the elementary doctrine of … repentance from dead works and of faith toward God'.[8]

This means it is impossible for someone to have true faith while defiantly refusing to repent of sin. In other words, it is impossible for someone to have Jesus as their Saviour if they will not have Him as their Lord. Either we do turn (*from* sin, *to* Jesus) or we don't turn. Describing how a person can be saved, Scripture often mentions faith without repentance. On other occasions it mentions repentance without faith.[9] Far from distancing the two, this illustrates the truth that one implies the other.

To be honest, I think my driving is brilliant. My wife begs to differ. The same goes for my navigation. (The main key to our long and happy marriage has been a Satnav.) However, I have to admit that over the years, I seem to have become weirdly adept at abrupt U-turns. From my expertise on this particular manoeuvre, I can safely say the following: Not once have I considered a U-turn complete when our car is ninety degrees to both lanes of traffic, facing directly across the road and blocking it; a scenario for the irate horn-sounding of others maybe, but not a complete turn. Only faith plus repentance – taking Jesus as both Saviour *and* Lord – amounts to a full turn from damnation to salvation.

4. Where do repentance and faith come from?

Another crucial feature of repentance and faith is that they are gifts to us from the God who enables us to carry them out. They are not in our fallen nature. Thomas Brooks describes this beautifully: 'Repentance is a flower which does not grow in nature's garden … [It] is a gift that comes down from above.'[10]

- To the Ephesians, Paul writes, 'For by grace you have been saved through faith. And this is not your own doing; it is the gift of God.'[11]

---

7. Acts 20:21.

8. Hebrews 6:1.

9. 2 Corinthians 7:10; Luke 24:46, 47; Acts 2:37, 38; Acts 3:19; Acts 5:31; Acts 17:30; Romans 2:4.

10. Thomas Brooks, *Precious Remedies Against Satan's Devices*.

11. Ephesians 2:8.

- To the Philippians Paul says that 'it has been granted to you that for the sake of Christ you should not only believe in him but also suffer for his sake'.[12]

- Peter addresses his readers, 'To those who have obtained a faith of equal standing with ours by the righteousness of our God and Saviour Jesus Christ.'[13]

- The writer to the Hebrews describes Jesus as 'the founder and perfecter of our faith'.[14]

- Luke records Peter's words about a man he healed: 'The faith that is through Jesus has given the man this perfect health.'[15]

Scripture often speaks of repentance or faith as our own actions, without referencing the underlying, divine grace from which those actions come. This reflects our genuine, live, personal responsibility to repent and trust. As we respond to God's call, we find ourselves gifted and empowered to obey. As Augustine prayed, 'Command what you will; grant what you command'.[16] Echo that simple prayer to reap wonderful fruit in your own life.

5. What is the place of repentance and faith in the Christian life?

On 31 October 1517, Martin Luther walked up to the Castle Church in Wittenberg and nailed a document to the doors. It was his ninety-five theses, arguments protesting against corruption in the Roman Catholic church. His hammer blows reverberate around the world to this day because they effectively launched the Protestant Reformation. The first of his ninety-five theses reads as follows: 'When our Lord and Master Jesus Christ said, "Repent," he willed the entire life of believers to be one of repentance.'

---

12. Philippians 1:29.
13. 2 Peter 1:1.
14. Hebrews 12:2.
15. Acts 3:16.
16. *The Confessions of St Augustine*, Book 9, Chapter 29, §40.

Repentance and faith are the pathway as well as the gateway of the Christian life. They are the way on as well as the way in. 'Be zealous and repent' Jesus commands Christians in Laodicea.[17] 'The life I now live in the flesh I live by faith in the Son of God' says Paul of his own Christian life.[18] 'Forgive us our sins' Jesus teaches His disciples to pray regularly, entailing both repentance and faith.[19]

When a young bird flies the nest for the first time, it needs to spread and pump its wings. But that isn't a one-time action guaranteeing a subsequent lifetime of flight. Using one's wings is the constant, ongoing requirement for a future of soaring freedom. Repentance and faith are the wings of the Christian life.

Have a good flight.

Prayer:

Loving Father, thank you for the doorway into everlasting life of repentance and faith. Thank you for your Word's clarity on these vital responses to your gospel. Thank you for your gift of them to me. Thank you for their eternal results. Please, for your name's sake, sustain them in me every single day of my life on this earth. In the name of the One who calls me to repent, and in whom I can put my faith, Amen.

Meditation:

Which aspect of the single turn are you more conscious of in your own life, repentance or faith? Why do you think this is?

---

17. Revelation 3:19.
18. Galatians 2:20.
19. Luke 11:4.

Act III
Life From The Cross

Day 11
The God Who Dies: Atonement

The moment we repent and believe, the benefits of the cross are applied to us. But what did it cost Jesus to win these blessings for us? What was occurring on the cross spiritually? And what exactly *are* the benefits of Jesus' death which we receive upon conversion?

The cross was planned by the Trinity from before the beginning of the world.[1] Yet when the time eventually came for its fulfilment, Scripture notably doesn't draw attention to the practical details. This is partly because crucifixion was well-known in the ancient world. To describe it in detail would have been redundant. In addition, focusing overly on the visible, physical suffering of the cross would have distracted from its deepest significance. However, what Jesus experienced bodily does have essential theological and practical importance for us.[2] Therefore some brief historical context, while grim, is appropriate.

---

1. Revelation 13:8.

2. One example of the **theological importance** of the intensely physical nature of Jesus' sufferings and death is found in our need for a valid substitute: 'Since therefore the children share in flesh and blood, *he himself likewise partook of the same things*, that through death he might destroy the one who has the power of death, that is, the devil' (Heb. 2:14). Our salvation hangs on (among other things) the fact that Jesus suffered and died according to His flesh and blood. As Peter puts it, 'He himself bore our sins *in his body* on the tree ... By his *wounds* you have been healed' (1 Pet. 2:24).
Peter also gives an example of the **practical importance** of Jesus' physical suffering: 'Since therefore Christ *suffered in the flesh*, arm yourselves with the same way of thinking, for whoever has *suffered in the flesh* has ceased from sin' (1 Pet. 4:1). Peter develops this argument in the following verses, but the point is that being aware of Jesus' suffering is powerful in our battle against sin.

Invented by the Persians and later perfected by the Romans, crucifixion was ingeniously designed to inflict maximum pain for a maximum length of time – sometimes days – before eventual death. Victims would be crucified naked, and in the rare case of women, facing the cross. Typically, five to seven-inch metal spikes would be inserted through the victims' wrists into the patibulum (crossbar). They would then be hoisted up on the stipes (vertical beam), impaled through the feet, and left to die of gradual asphyxiation. Victims would find themselves needing to push up with their arms and legs in order to open the chest cavity to breathe. When their strength eventually failed, they would suffocate. This is why, if the executioners wanted to hasten death for some practical reason, a simple solution was to break the victims' legs.

Other suffering included the possibility of crows pecking out the eyes of still-living victims, excruciating nerve pain from the impalements, muscle spasms, and shoulder dislocations. In addition, there would be searing, trauma-induced thirst, and the grind of the writhing victim's flogged back against the rough timber of the upright beam. The final agonies would include the crushing pain of the pericardium starting to fill with fluid and compress the heart.

Added to Jesus' physical suffering was the mental suffering of His anticipation of crucifixion,[3] the relational suffering of His closest friends' betrayal and abandonment,[4] and the emotional suffering of His humiliation:[5] as well as His public nakedness He would have experienced pain-induced incontinence. Yet there were three even more profound and significant agonies.

First, on the cross, the spotlessly innocent One had chosen to take all the guilt for all the sins of all the people who would ever be saved. 'The Lord has laid on him the iniquity of us all.'[6] The trauma for the sinless One of taking ownership of such an immeasurable tonnage of sin is unthinkable. Imagine the most hygienically-conscious man in the world going swimming in a swimming pool of diarrhoea, rubbing

---

3. Luke 22:42-44.

4. Matthew 26:56.

5. Philippians 2:8.

6. Isaiah 53:6.

it into his face and hair and swilling it around his mouth. The dazzling purity of Christ's holiness and the appalling depths of our sin make even that analogy inadequate. '[God] made him to be sin who knew no sin …'[7]

Second, entailed in the Son's choice to take on His people's guilt was His absorption of the Father's righteous, burning fury for that guilt. He was facing holy, divine, exploding rage for all of the sins that His countless millions of people in history would ever repent of. He was guilty of all the child abuse. All the racism. All the rapes. All the abortions. All the lies. All the blasphemy. All the idolatry. All the arrogance. All the broken promises. All the selfishness. All of the everything. 'He was pierced for our transgressions; he was crushed for our iniquities … It was the will of the Lord to crush him.'[8]

Third, these last two agonies meant the existential suffering of Jesus' isolation – the sudden, violent dislocation of His earthly relationship with His Father.[9] 'My God, my God, why have you forsaken me?' came His jagged scream.[10] The One who had known only joyful intimacy with His beloved Father from eternity past, whose Father had been His supreme joy in a life of sorrow, was suddenly, brutally severed from Him. He suffered with an aching intensity of aloneness which we will never understand.

But after six hours, Jesus was able to roar in triumph, 'It is finished!'[11] On the cross, Jesus drank to its dregs the combined judgement of all the eternities in hell which all of God's people across human history would have suffered for their sins. Jesus didn't come down off the cross with His people's judgement only partially taken. 'He loved them to the end.'[12] His mission was completed.

So how should we view the cross? Where does it fit within the bigger picture of our faith?

---

7. 2 Corinthians 5:21.

8. Isaiah 53:5, 10.

9. Psalm 22:1.

10. Mark 15:34. In quoting the first line of Psalm 22 in this way, Jesus was referencing the whole psalm, which contains a remarkable set of prophecies about the nature of His death, as well as an inspiring commentary on its significance.

11. John 19:30.

12. John 13:1.

The cross is the essence of Christianity. It is the apex of God's glory, the zenith of His revelation, the centrepiece of His plan for the universe. 'I decided to know nothing among you' wrote Paul to the distracted Corinthians, 'except Jesus Christ and him crucified.'[13] Calvin said 'There is no tribunal so magnificent, no throne so stately, no show of triumph so distinguished, no chariot so elevated, as is the gibbet on which Christ hath subdued death and the devil.'[14] At the heart of the Christian faith is the cross. And at the heart of the cross, the heart of the heart as it were, is penal substitutionary atonement.

'Penal' means Jesus took the penalty, the punishment for our sin. 'Substitutionary' means He did so in our place, taking our guilt and granting us His righteousness. 'Atonement' refers to the resulting restoration of our relationship with God, the closing of the chasm. Think of atonement as 'at-one-ment'.

Penal substitutionary atonement appears frequently in Scripture. An obvious example is 1 Peter 3:18. Note the penal element in line one, the substitution in line two and the atonement in line three:

> For Christ also suffered once for sins,
> the righteous for the unrighteous,
> that he might bring us to God.

Yet so much more was occurring on the cross as well. In the chapters that follow, we'll consider four of the central results of Jesus' death, which are key to the atonement: propitiation, justification, redemption and adoption. Further blessings of the cross include our reconciliation and unity with each other,[15] our marching orders for the Christian life,[16] our proof of God's inexhaustible love and ongoing provision,[17] victory over Satan and his demons,[18] and God's supreme revelation to us of Himself.[19] Even this survey falls far short of all that the

---

13. 1 Corinthians 2:2.

14. See John Calvin's comment on Colossians 2:15 in *The Epistles of Paul the Apostle to the Philippians, Colossians and Thessalonians*, Calvin's Commentaries (Grand Rapids, MI: Eerdmans, 1996).

15. Ephesians 2:14; Colossians 1:20.

16. Matthew 16:24; John 13:34.

17. Romans 8:32.

18. Colossians 2:14, 15; 1 John 3:8.

19. 1 Corinthians 1:23, 24.

cross achieved.[20] The death of Jesus Christ is infinitely profound and precious. What are we to take for now from Jesus' death for us?

Penal

Be sobered by the seriousness of your sin, that it should cost Jesus the penalty of such fathomless suffering: 'And being in an agony [at the prospect of the suffering described above] he prayed more earnestly; and his sweat became like great drops of blood falling down to the ground.'[21]

Substitutionary

Rejoice and be secure in Jesus' love for you. As well as obedience to His Father's will,[22] and commitment to His Father's glory, it was the limitless heights of His love for you personally which compelled Him to become your substitute. He is 'the Son of God who loved me and gave himself for me'.[23]

Atonement

Embrace in worship the Father to whom you have been reconciled. You have been welcomed in. Your atonement is complete. 'But now in Christ Jesus you who once were far off [from God] have been brought near by the blood of Christ.'[24]

Prayer:

Merciful Father, I praise you for the gift of your Son and His willing sacrifice. Grant me for the rest of my days an ever-deepening love and understanding of the cross. Help me keep it as the centrepiece of my life, and to cling to it with repentance, faith, joy and worship. In the name of the One who gave His life for me, Amen.

Meditation:

How would you sum up the essential achievement of the cross in one sentence?

---

20. See for example John Piper's *Fifty Reasons Why Jesus Came to Die* (Crossway, 2006).

21. Luke 22:44.

22. Luke 22:42.

23. Galatians 2:20.

24. Ephesians 2:13.

Day 12

The God Who Satisfies His Wrath: Propitiation

I'll never forget leaning out of an upstairs window at school, lobbing a sodden toilet roll into the courtyard below, and being caught red- (or in fact soggy) handed by a teacher. His exasperation was palpable. I knew a punishment would be quickly heading my way. However, what hit me hardest was the justified, heated anger from a kind, fair adult who I respected. His ire was controlled but awful. (Mr Baker, if you ever read these words, I really was sorry.)

One reason we can be ignorant and under-appreciative of the doctrine of propitiation is that we underestimate the seriousness of God's holy fury at our sin. 'Who can endure the heat of his anger?' asks the Prophet Nahum. 'His wrath is poured out like fire, and the rocks are broken into pieces by him.'[1]

We might be tempted to think God is too heavy on sin. But if so, we need to admit our vested interest in seeing sin as less serious than it is, our sin-distorted perception of sin, and our underestimation of God's holiness. Martyn Lloyd-Jones observes, 'You will never make yourself feel that you are a sinner, because there is a mechanism in you as a result of sin that will always be defending you … We are all on very good terms with ourselves.'[2] We don't understand the seriousness of our sin because of … our sin! A glimpse of anything even close to the dizzying heights of God's divine goodness would reveal something of

---

1. Nahum 1:6.

2. Martyn Lloyd-Jones, *Seeking the Face of God: Nine Reflections on the Psalms* (Crossway, 2005), p. 34.

the plunging abyss of our wickedness. Puritan Thomas Goodwin, who was renowned for his emphasis on the tender love of God, admits the awful truth: If 'his wrath against sin was the fire, [then] ... all earthly bellows would ... not have been able to make the furnace hot enough'.[3] Rather than God being too heavy on our sin, it is we who are too light. His wrath is righteous, necessary and inevitable.[4]

It must therefore somehow be dealt with if He is to be able to accept us. The anger must still occur of course, for it would be immoral and therefore impossible for Him not to express it. But for Him to have a relationship with us, His wrath must be expressed in a way that doesn't involve our destruction. As Jesus hung on the cross, He was satisfying, appeasing, quenching, exhausting that fury. He was, in John's words, 'the propitiation for our sins'.[5]

Picture a lightning rod. The lightning of God's anger at sin, once released, must land somewhere. The cross is the divine conductor, lovingly supplied by the Father and willingly enacted by the Son. Christ gladly absorbs the holy strike for the sake of His people's safety.

Or picture a sandbag. The soldier crouches behind it as the bullet flies towards him. At the last millisecond, the projectile's kinetic energy is quenched. The sandbag is pierced. The bullet is spent. The soldier's life is preserved.

Or picture a cup. This is the Old Testament image Christ Himself went to in the garden, contemplating the agonies to come. In Jerry Bridges' words, 'Christ exhausted the cup of God's wrath. For all who trust in him there is nothing more in the cup. It is empty.'[6]

Yet the idea of propitiation hasn't always been popular in church history. Until seven hundred years ago, there was no English word for adequately translating the Bible's Greek word *hilasterion*. Some have tried to translate it simply as 'sacrifice' in an effort to make Scripture's language more accessible. However, that simply isn't what *hilasterion*

---

3. Thomas Goodwin, *Of Gospel Holiness in the Heart and Life*, in *The Works of Thomas Goodwin*, 12 vols. (repr., Reformation Heritage, 2006), 7:194.

4. I am grateful for the outline of this argument and the Lloyd-Jones and Goodwin quotations, to Dane Ortlund's *Gentle and Lowly: The Heart of Christ for Sinners and Sufferers* (Crossway, 2020), pp. 67, 68.

5. 1 John 2:2.

6. Jerry Bridges, *The Gospel for Real Life* (NavPress, 2002).

means.[7] Others have wanted to translate it 'expiation' which means the removal of sin. Wonderfully, expiation *has* of course happened. It's happened 'as far as the east is from the west'![8] But once again, that's not the meaning of *hilasterion*.

Sometimes these mistranslations have been deliberate, to avoid the concept of propitiation, by those who object to the idea of a wrathful instead of loving Father. But is anger really mutually exclusive with love? If you were to harm my son, and I were to respond, 'No problem. I don't mind', would you conclude that I was loving? Far from denying my love, my wrath would demonstrate and prove it. God's anger reassures us of His fierce love for the victims of sin. 'Beloved, never avenge yourselves, but leave it to the wrath of God, for it is written, "Vengeance is mine, I will repay, says the Lord."'[9]

Even more importantly, His wrath also reassures us of His commitment to His own glory. Paul explains: 'For the wrath of God is revealed from heaven against all ungodliness and unrighteousness of men, who by their unrighteousness suppress the truth [about His attributes and nature – that is, His glory].'[10]

Others have also objected that propitiation implies a God who insists on being bribed grotesquely out of His anger. This is the case with pagan deities, but the Christian God could not be more different: their anger is cruel and capricious while His is holy and settled. They demand that propitiation be given in a crude bargain for resumed blessing, whereas alongside the Lord's requirement for propitiation is His gracious, loving, self-sacrificial provision. He doesn't only demand propitiation *from* us. He then provides it *for* us! Jesus, as Paul says, was the One 'whom God put forward as a propitiation by his blood'.[11]

---

7. 'The general meaning of the word is the appeasing of the wrath of the Deity by prayer or sacrifice when a sin or offence has been committed against Him ... Such a translation accurately represents the meaning in classical Greek of the words used (*hilasterion, hilasmos*).' *The Oxford Dictionary of the Christian Church* (Oxford University Press, 2005).

8. Psalm 103:12.

9. Romans 12:19.

10. Romans 1:18.

11. Romans 3:25.

This also means that we must never picture propitiation as some intra-trinitarian rift as the Father and the Son pull in the opposite directions of wrath and love and the Son pleads with the Father to love us.[12] Propitiation *is* the Father's love to us, expressed in His provision of His willing Son to achieve it. 'He loved us and sent his Son to be the propitiation for our sins.'[13]

To this day, Jesus our advocate successfully presents our case to His joyful Father, based not on our perfection, but His propitiation. A lawyer friend tells me how vital it is for people in his profession to know their cases. It's safe to say this advocate knows His case: this advocate *is* His case! In John's words, 'If anyone does sin, we have an advocate with the Father, Jesus Christ the righteous. *He is* the propitiation for our sins.'[14]

Yet not only is Jesus our propitia*tion*. He is also our propitia*tor*. Not only is He the sacrifice. He is also the One who offered the sacrifice. He is 'a merciful and faithful high priest ... to make propitiation for the sins of the people'.[15] Truly, God has gone before and completed everything for us.

As you go about life today, praise God for the evidence of His holy fury that harm to His creatures and defamation of His character *does* matter to Him.

Be sobered at the seriousness of your sin: nothing less than the propitiation of God's beloved Son was required to deal with His righteous anger at it.

Be humble and joyful that the Father and Son should willingly provide, in love, such costly propitiation.

And let your love today for your brothers and sisters in Christ follow the example of your Father's love for you: practical, radical and self-giving. 'In this is love, not that we have loved God but that he loved us and sent his Son to be the propitiation for our sins.'[16]

---

12. Not that these *are* opposite directions anyway. See the example above of my reaction to my son being harmed.

13. 1 John 4:10.

14. 1 John 2:1, 2.

15. Hebrews 2:17.

16. 1 John 4:10.

Prayer:

Father, thank you for your loving provision of your willing Son as my propitiation. Thank you for sparing me from your holy wrath at sin, at more personal cost than I will ever know. Help me to rejoice in this doctrine, to be humbled and sobered by it, and to show my fellow believers the same kind of love as the love from you which it demonstrates. In the name of Christ my propitiator and advocate, Amen.

Meditation:

How would you summarise the meaning of propitiation in one simple sentence? Which of the implications of it examined here strikes you the most? Why?

Day 13
The God Who Declares Righteous: Justification

Before his conversion, John Bunyan was the ringleader of his rough group of friends. As well as being exceptionally foul-mouthed, he was infamous for the energy he channelled into what the seventeenth century described, tamely to our ears, as 'mischief'. He became secretly disturbed by these things, but found himself helpless to change. He later wrote in his autobiography:

> One day as I was passing into the field, suddenly this sentence fell upon my soul: 'Thy righteousness is in heaven.' And with the eyes of my soul I saw Jesus at the Father's right hand. 'There,' I said, 'is my righteousness!' So that wherever I was or whatever I was doing, God could not say to me, 'Where is your righteousness?' For it is always right before him. I saw that it is not my good frame of heart that made my righteousness better, nor yet my bad frame that made my righteousness worse, for my righteousness is Christ. Now my chains fell off indeed. My temptations fled away, and I lived sweetly at peace with God.[1]

Bunyan was describing the doctrine of justification, won for us on the cross. The Westminster Shorter Catechism defines justification as 'an act of God's free grace wherein he pardons all our sins and accepts us as righteous in his sight only for the righteousness of Christ imputed to us and received by faith alone'.[2]

Scripture is clear on each of these elements.

---

1. John Bunyan, *Grace Abounding to the Chief of Sinners*, p.229.
2. Westminster Shorter Catechism, Question 33.

- We are 'justified *by his grace*',[3] that is, His unmerited kindness.

- We are pardoned: 'Who shall bring any charge against God's elect? It is God who justifies. Who is to condemn?'[4]

- Our guilt is not only expunged but replaced with Jesus' righteousness: 'For our sake he [God] made him to be sin who knew no sin, so that in him we might become the righteousness of God.'[5]

- Christ's righteousness is credited to us because of our faith, not because of our works: 'And to the one who...believes in him who justifies the ungodly, his faith is counted as righteousness.'[6]

Justification is a legal term. It pictures God as the judge in heaven's law court pronouncing a verdict upon us of 'not guilty', as well as declaring us perfectly righteous. The obvious consequence of this for us is eternal life. We are confidently able to stand in the presence of a holy God and survive. He is joyfully able to accept us instead of having to destroy us. 'Since we have been justified by faith, we have peace with God.'[7] Yet beyond this, the implications of justification run far and wide.[8] For example, this doctrine leads us to ...

... godliness. As Bunyan found, being convinced of our status of righteousness is a powerful impetus for living it out. This is why Paul can speak of putting off our old self, being renewed in our minds – that is, understanding what God has done for us and understanding our resulting new status – and *therefore* 'put[ting] on the new self,

---

3. Romans 3:24.

4. Romans 8:33, 34.

5. 2 Corinthians 5:21.

6. Romans 4:5.

7. Romans 5:1.

8. Applications of justification not examined here include but are not limited to: assurance, thanksgiving, a guard against racism, a healthy relationship with failure, and a godly approach to work. The practical implications of justification by faith are practically endless and life-changing.

created after the likeness of God in true righteousness and holiness'.[9] When entangled in a particular sin, focus on the reality that your true status is one of innocence and freedom from that sin. Frame the battle in terms of fighting to be who you are instead of living the lie of someone you are not.

... peace. Justification grants us peace with God, in contrast to the former state of war between us and Him because of our guilt. 'Therefore, since we have been justified by faith, we have peace with God through our Lord Jesus Christ.'[10] As Bunyan described, this objective peace leads to subjective peace as we experience a sense of relief and reconciliation with God. Acknowledge and enjoy the sensation of being at one with your Maker, accepted joyfully by Him and able to rest in Him.

... humility. 'Christ Jesus ... became to us wisdom from God, righteousness [the same word as justification in New Testament Greek] and sanctification and redemption, so that, as it is written, "Let the one who boasts, boast in the Lord."'[11]

Justification is available only in Christ, not ourselves. It is received only by faith in Him, not by our works.[12] Therefore any boasting or self-congratulation for our salvation is farcically inappropriate. As Puritan Thomas Watson said, 'God does not justify us because we are worthy, but by justifying us makes us worthy'.[13] Let God's justification drive you instead to humble worship rather than self-congratulation.

... equality. Justification is a binary state. It does not apply to some believers more than others. The most inexperienced or spiritually frail or sin-riddled Christian is no less justified than any other. The Apostle Paul himself had been responsible for the murder of Christians, and described himself as 'chief of sinners' yet rejoiced in his salvation with

---

9. Ephesians 4:24.

10. Romans 5:1.

11. 1 Corinthians 1:30, 31.

12. Galatians 2:16.

13. Thomas Watson, 'Body of Divinity: The Application of Redemption', Question 23 under 'Justification'.

no hint of insecurity.[14] The Apostle Peter could write 'To those who have obtained a faith *of equal standing with ours* by the righteousness [that is, justification] of our God and Saviour Jesus Christ.'[15] Justification is the great spiritual leveller. Let God's justification guard you from any self-delusional inferiority complex towards other believers. The ground at the foot of the cross is level.

... defence against spiritual attack. 'God made [you] alive together with him, having forgiven us all our trespasses, by cancelling the record of debt that stood against us with its legal demands. This he set aside, nailing it to the cross. He disarmed the rulers and authorities and put them to open shame, by triumphing over them in him.'[16]

The rulers and authorities in view here are demonic powers, and their potency against people comes from feeding off human sin. By cancelling and setting aside your sin (as happens in justification), God disarmed them and removed their ground for preying on you. If you sense the possibility of demonic influence in your life through strangely intensified temptation, discouragement, doubt, or a loss of personal control, claim the freedom from these attacks available for you in justification.

...mission. A main purpose of Paul's letter to the Romans is to motivate them to support his missionary work.[17] At the heart of the letter is the doctrine of justification by faith. How are these linked?

'That is why it [justification] depends on faith, in order that the promise may rest on grace and be guaranteed to all his [Abraham's] offspring – not only to the adherent of the law but also to the one who shares the faith of Abraham, who is the father of us all, as it is written, "I have made you the father of many nations"'.[18]

If justification was available only to those who had faith *and* kept the Mosaic law, most of the world would be discounted.[19] Whereas

---

14. 1 Timothy 1:15.
15. 2 Peter 1:1.
16. Colossians 2:13-15.
17. Romans 15:24.
18. Romans 4:16, 17.
19. Romans 4:11, 12.

justification in fact 'depends on faith'. This throws open the doors of salvation to any and all who call upon the name of Jesus. As well as being the great spiritual leveller (see above, under 'equality'), justification by faith is also the great missiological leveller. As you reach out in love to the lost around you, be encouraged: regardless of any conceivable personal situation or background, the only thing anyone needs for everlasting life is simple faith. No one is beyond the reach of God's merciful justification.

Prayer:

Holy and merciful God, I praise you for pronouncing me innocent of guilt and instead righteous with Christ's own righteousness. Thank you Father for this unimpeachable declaration. Thank you Lord Jesus for enabling it by your blood.[20] Thank you Spirit for applying it by your power.[21] Grant me to drink deep of the truth of justification, for my blessing and your glory. In the name of the One whose righteousness has become my own, enabling me to come into your presence with this prayer, Amen.

Meditation:

Which of the implications of justification mentioned in this chapter is most needful in your life right now? Why?

---

20. Romans 5:9.

21. 1 Corinthians 6:11.

Day 14

The God Who Sets Free:
Redemption

A. J. Gordon was a pastor in Boston in the 1880s. The story is told of a boy walking past him carrying a wire cage in which some small birds fluttered anxiously. 'Where did you get those birds?' Gordon asked. The boy had trapped them in a nearby field and was heading home to toy with them before feeding them to his cat. Gordon offered to purchase them. 'Mister, they're just little old birds and can't even sing very well!' But Gordon persisted, offering the boy two dollars for the birds and cage. 'OK, deal' said the boy, 'but you're making a bad bargain!' Gordon smiled, walked behind his church building, and then opened the cage door. He gazed as the creatures soared up into the blue.

The following Sunday he took the cage into the pulpit and used it to illustrate the truth of redemption – how Jesus came to rescue the lost, paying with His blood as a ransom to set them free. Gordon finished with these words: 'That boy told me the birds were not songsters. But when I released them and they winged their way heavenward, it seemed to me as if they were singing, "Redeemed, redeemed, redeemed!"'[1]

To redeem means to purchase from slavery, to rescue from captivity, to buy back, to set free. Listen to Jesus: 'For even the Son of Man came not to be served but to serve, *and to give his life as a ransom for many.*'[2] 'Everyone who practices sin is a slave to sin ... So if the Son sets you free, you will be free indeed.'[3]

---

1. Source unknown.
2. Mark 10:45.
3. John 8:34, 36.

And this redemption is a rich theme throughout Scripture. In the Old Testament, we see God's people redeemed from a wide variety of enemies including debt, captivity, slavery, exile and capital punishment. Scripture's focus then narrows to spiritual realities in the New Testament, and we read about our redemption in three ways in particular.

The first is redemption from our guilt. 'In him we have redemption through his blood, the forgiveness of our trespasses.'[4] Jesus' death set us free from our trespasses by paying for them, enabling God's forgiveness of them. His blood allowed God's justice and holiness to be fulfilled, instead of our guilt being quietly brushed under the carpet (an impossibility). It enabled the Father to forgive and accept us, without compromising His character (an impossibility).

Second, the New Testament says we are redeemed from condemnation before God's perfect moral standards. 'Christ redeemed us from the curse of the law by becoming a curse for us—for it is written, "Cursed is everyone who is hanged on a tree."'[5] This is the curse from God on all who reject and defy Him by breaking His law. Because He is infinitely majestic and worthy of honour, dishonouring Him is infinitely serious. This in turn means that its consequences are infinitely serious: everlasting damnation. That is the curse from which Jesus sets us free.

Third, Christ redeems us from futility – the futility of trying to deal with our sin ourselves. We are like a drowning seabird covered in oil from a spillage, frantically trying to clean itself off as it drowns. Christ sets us free from that struggle by rescuing and washing us Himself. 'You were ransomed from the futile ways inherited from your forefathers, not with perishable things such as silver or gold, but with the precious blood of Christ.'[6] Ever since the Fall, humanity has been constantly, frantically trying to cover up our crimes and atone for their consequences. Everything we've tried in thousands of years has proved futile. It's all been one exhausting, endless, fruitless effort. Jesus has saved us from that futility.

---

4. Ephesians 1:7.
5. Galatians 3:13.
6. 1 Peter 1:18, 19.

These three past senses of redemption give cause in turn to a future sense. Writing about the coming New Creation, Paul describes eagerly *awaiting* 'the redemption of our bodies'.[7] Our past redemption from sin's guilt and penalty and power enables our future redemption from sin's presence and effects. The entire created order will be gloriously renewed. This will include our physical bodies, which will be set free forever from their aches and pains and diseases and disabilities and tiredness and mortality. Praise God for that coming 'Day of Redemption'.[8]

One implication of all this is that we can fight and flee from sin with re-doubled motivation. Having been redeemed from sin, failing to flee is like being released from the birdcage but then flying back into it. It's like breaking back into the death row prison from which I had been set free and continuing to live in the old cell, eat the disgusting food, lie on the hard bed, pull the flea-infested blanket over me, and start waiting once again for execution.

Here is how Peter describes this:

> For whatever overcomes a person, to that he is enslaved. For if, after they have escaped the defilements of the world through the knowledge of our Lord and Saviour Jesus Christ, they are again entangled in them and overcome, the last state has become worse for them than the first. For it would have been better for them never to have known the way of righteousness than after knowing it to turn back … What the true proverb says has happened to them: 'The dog returns to its own vomit, and the sow, after washing herself, returns to wallow in the mire.'[9]

You've been set free. Feel your liberty. Treasure it. Chase your sanctification. Fly!

Another implication of redemption is to worship the Redeemer. Just as being redeemed *from sin* drives us to *sanctification*, so being redeemed *by Christ* drives us to *devotion*. He is our focus, our love, our life, our freedom. Hear this logic in our worship in eternity:

---

7. Romans 8:23.

8. Ephesians 4:30.

9. 2 Peter 2:19-22. Although Peter here is talking specifically about false teachers, the principle surely extends to any apparent believer who fits Peter's chilling description in these verses.

And they sang a new song, saying, 'Worthy are you [Jesus] to take the scroll and open its seals [that is, fulfil God's purposes], for you were slain, and *by your blood you ransomed people for God ...'* ... Then I looked, and I heard ... the voice of many angels, numbering myriads of myriads and thousands of thousands, saying with a loud voice, 'Worthy is the Lamb who was slain, to receive power and wealth and wisdom and might and honour and glory and blessing!'[10]

As you continue to soar from the cage, don't forget to keep singing. It's what you were set free for. It's what will fulfil you. And your Redeemer deserves and enjoys it.

Prayer:

Dear Father, I praise you for sending your precious Son to set me free by His blood shed on the cross. Thank you for my redemption from guilt and condemnation and futility. Thank you for the future redemption of my body and with it the whole world. Empower me to experience and make the most of my freedom by continuing my flight from sin without looking back. And fill my heart with ever increasing joy and thankfulness and admiration of your Son, my Redeemer. In His name I pray, Amen.

Meditation:

Which are your 'signature sins', the sins you are most prone to in this season? Do you see the wilful committing of them as an attempted return to captivity and condemnation? How does the doctrine of redemption give you motivation and encouragement in your ongoing battle with them?

---

10. Revelation 5:9, 11, 12.

Day 15
The God Who Brings Home: Adoption

You're standing in a large room. The acrid stench of soiled bedding hits your nostrils. The sound of buzzing flies joins with the occasional scuttle of a rat and the faint whimpering coming from the rows of cots in front of you – whimpering, not full-blooded crying, because the babies and toddlers have learnt that only rarely will anyone come.

You reflect on the twelve-month process which has taken you to this point: research, phone calls, paperwork, meetings with lawyers, financial payments, the arrangement of time off work back in your own country, vaccinations, flight bookings, hotel bookings, orphanage visits, more financial payments, meetings with officials, court hearings – the list seems interminable. And yet here you stand. An hour ago, a judge finally granted the longed-for adoption order. Now is the fulfilment of a year's endeavour.

You reach down into the cot in front of you, and scoop up the little girl with whom you've been bonding in recent weeks. You enfold her in a clean, soft blanket, and tenderly whisper her new name over her. Next stop, the airport. She is finally yours to bring home.

You are that baby.

You were an orphan in the universe, hopeless and helpless, living out a tragedy.[1] When your Father had fulfilled all that was needed – an extraordinary, miraculous process of propitiation, justification and redemption, planned from eternity past and accomplished on the cross – He was finally able to reach down, scoop you up and bring you

---

1. John 14:18.

home. Welcome to the doctrine of adoption. Welcome to the family. Welcome home.

Paul said it like this:

> For all who are led by the Spirit of God are sons of God. For you did not receive the spirit of slavery to fall back into fear, but you have received the Spirit of adoption as sons, by whom we cry, 'Abba! Father!' The Spirit himself bears witness with our spirit that we are children of God.[2]

Yet we can struggle to accept the reality of our adoption in practice. Consider Dane Ortlund's words:

> There are two ways to live the Christian life. You can live it either *for* the heart of Christ or *from* the heart of Christ ... *For* a new identity as a son or daughter of God or *from* it. The battle of the Christian life is to bring your own heart into alignment with Christ's, that is, getting up each morning and replacing your natural orphan mind-set with a mind-set of full and free adoption into the family of God.[3]

We don't need to live *for* a place in God's family – we already have that! We don't need to live *for* gaining the God of the universe as our own Father – we already have that! Slipping unconsciously into living the Christian life that way round will lead only to resentment, insecurity, exhaustion and joyless legalism. No amount of spiritual or moral achievement could ever earn God's adoption. However, simply dwelling on some of the privileges involved in our adoption helps drive its reality deeper into our hearts. Here are some of those privileges:[4]

We can speak to the Creator of the universe as our personal Father. Don't lose sight of the truth that praying 'Our Father' is an astonishing honour.[5] More than just your maker, sustainer, master, judge, teacher, provider and protector, God is also your Daddy.

We receive the Spirit's inward witness, causing us to know God as our Father. 'You have received the Spirit of adoption as sons, by

---

2. Romans 8:14-16.

3. Dane Ortlund, *Gentle and Lowly: The Heart of Christ for Sinners and Sufferers* (Crossway, 2020), p. 181.

4. Wayne Grudem lists some of these privileges in *Systematic Theology: An Introduction to Biblical Doctrine* (IVP, 1994), pp. 739-742.

5. Matthew 6:9.

whom we cry, "Abba! Father!" The Spirit himself bears witness with our spirit that we are children of God."[6] I once saw a video of some ducklings who believed a kindly golden retriever to be their father, and treated him as such, following him everywhere. Not for us that confusion. As a believer, your instinct that God is your Father isn't conditioned or coincidental or cultural. The third person of the Trinity placed it in you.

We receive good gifts in response to requests to our Father. 'If you then, who are evil, know how to give good gifts to your children, how much more will your Father who is in heaven give good things to those who ask him!'[7] Your Father isn't stingy or absent or passive or harsh or inept. Being God, He is a perfect Father. He is a joyfully, bountifully, overflowingly generous Father. He loves to hear your requests, and when they are for your best, to grant them. Don't miss out on this privilege!

We can look forward to an eternal inheritance from our Father. Paul points out that as God's children, we are God's heirs.[8] This gives us access, in Peter's description, to 'an inheritance that is imperishable, undefiled, and unfading, kept in heaven for you'.[9] This will include being given authority to rule with Christ over the nations, in the New Creation.[10] Being a child of the King means you are on the brink of receiving staggering honours.

We get to be disciplined by our wise and loving Father. 'The Lord disciplines the one he loves, and chastises every son whom he receives.'[11] You do not have a Father who will spoil or overindulge you, leaving you fragile, immature and unattractive. You have a Father who will carefully, tenderly correct you for the sake of your character and spiritual health, because He loves you. When life is painful, don't be resentful or discouraged. Be considering why your Father may be needing to grab your attention sharply in a particular area of life. And

---

6. Romans 8:15, 16.

7. Matthew 7:11.

8. Galatians 4:7.

9. 1 Peter 1:4.

10. Revelation 2:26, 27; 3:21.

11. Hebrews 12:6.

if you perceive divine discipline in your circumstances, be grateful. He is training you because He cares about you. You will be healthier and wiser and ultimately more joyful for it.

We gain a worldwide family of brothers and sisters. When Jesus' disciples were anxiously contemplating the fact they had left everything to follow Him, Jesus encouraged them with these words:

> There is no one who has left house or brothers or sisters or mother or father or children or lands, for my sake and for the gospel, who will not receive a hundredfold now in this time, houses and brothers and sisters and mothers and children and lands, with persecutions, and in the age to come eternal life.[12]

Being brought into your Father's family gains you millions of beautiful siblings, your fellow adoptees. In addition, your own church is also a family within the family. You will never be cut off from Christian kindness and support in this world. You will never be lacking for care and encouragement of fellow believers in this life. You will never have to walk alone.

Prayer:

Abba! Thank you for your kindness and love in adopting me. Thank you for the privileges entailed in being your child. Help me to embrace them for my joy and your glory. Would your adoption of me sink ever deeper into my heart, that I may live not for it but from it! In the name of my older brother and co-heir, the Lord Jesus, Amen.

Meditation:

What could be signs of slipping into living for being a son or daughter of God instead of from that status?

---

12. Mark 10:29, 30.

Day 16

The God Who Rises: Resurrection

Have you ever wondered why the Father made His Son's resurrection so spectacular? Why the earthquake, the angels looking like lightning, and the resurrections of other believers from tombs around Jerusalem?[1] None of those things were functionally necessary for Jesus to be brought back to life.

The resurrection was spectacular because the meaning of the resurrection is spectacular. The Father wanted the resurrection emblazoned and celebrated because while not less than a physical, historical event, it was also much more. More than simply a nice, neat 'happily ever after' ending to Jesus' earthly ministry, the resurrection adds to the saving blessings of the cross many further blessings, in the form of proofs and authentications.

These include the authentication of: our own future resurrections, the coming judgement,[2] the goal of our faith,[3] the fact that we have a living Saviour,[4] and the fact that our hope is a living hope rather than a dead hope for this world only.[5] Five further assurances which we have space to explore now include:

The authentication of our new birth

'According to his great mercy, he [the Father] has caused us to be born again to a living hope through the resurrection of Jesus Christ.'[6] Jesus'

---

1. Matthew 27:52.
2. Acts 17:31.
3. 1 Corinthians 15:17.
4. Revelation 1:18.
5. 1 Peter 1:3; 1 Corinthians 15:19.
6. 1 Peter 1:3.

FROM EVERLASTING TO EVERLASTING

resurrection proves and illustrates the new life we received from the Father at the moment of our regeneration.

We will continue to experience sin and its effects until we receive our promised spiritual and physical perfection after this life. Nonetheless, we already have the new life with which Jesus rose! Without it, we couldn't right now be fellowshipping with God and living the Christian life. As Paul wrote, 'just as Christ was raised from the dead by the glory of the Father, we too might walk in newness of life.'[7] Be encouraged by the life that is yours even as you read these words.

The authentication of the success of Jesus' work on the cross

Jesus 'humbled himself by becoming obedient to the point of death, even death on a cross. *Therefore* God has highly exalted him'.[8] The resurrection demonstrated God's approval and vindication of Jesus' sacrifice. It showed God's people that the cross had been effective. This explains Paul's statement that '[Jesus] was delivered up for our trespasses and raised for our justification'.[9] He means not that the resurrection achieved our justification, but that following our justification, it proved and guaranteed that new status. The resurrection also does the same for the propitiation, redemption, adoption and all the other myriad things Christ won for us at His death.

Picture a rugby player crashing over the try line and successfully getting the ball down to score for his team. He is marmalised in the process by the opposition, but his actions win the game. In celebration, his team mates haul him to his feet and embrace him. The resurrection is the Father hauling the Son to His feet and embracing Him. If you are ever tempted to doubt whether you have been truly justified, look at the resurrection. Jesus' labours for us on Calvary were successful!

The authentication of the Father's power towards us

Paul prays for the Ephesian believers to know 'the immeasurable greatness of his power toward us who believe, according to the working of his great might that he worked in Christ when he raised him from the dead'.[10]

---

7. Romans 6:4.
8. Philippians 2:8, 9.
9. Romans 4:25.
10. Ephesians 1:19, 20.

If you want to picture the power of the Father, first picture the power of death. It is like a hideous ogre towering over us from the moment of birth, monstrous in size, inescapable, unstoppable, 'the last enemy',[11] the victor in countless billions of individual struggles since the world began. But now picture the Father towering over *him*, dwarfing *him*. And picture Him seizing the ogre in His hands, and quickly, deftly snapping his neck.

That is what the Father did for Jesus on the first Easter morning. If you are in Christ, that is what He has done for you. And if even death is no match for your Father's might, how much more can you entrust Him with anything else you're facing!

The authentication of our ability to resist sin

'For the death [Christ] died he died to sin, once for all, but the life he lives he lives to God. So you also must consider yourselves dead to sin and alive to God in Christ Jesus. Let not sin therefore reign in your mortal body.'[12] When we sin, we violently contradict our identity and status as those who have been raised spiritually and will be raised physically. To indulge in sin is to deny the resurrection life we now live.

When our golden retriever Charlie was a puppy, he had a disturbing penchant for gobbling up his own poop. There was always an alternative for him in that moment: cuddles, praise and delicious treats. What's more, on the occasions he opted for these instead, they obviously gave him much greater happiness than his self-catering. Yet sometimes his chronic irrationality overrode his awareness of his identity and status, and the wonderful implications for him of those things. (That's how he put it to me anyway.) Sin is inherently irrational. You have been given new resurrection life. Don't eat your poop.

The authentication of the significance of our labours for Christ

Following a discussion of the resurrection, Paul exclaims, '*Therefore*, my beloved brothers, be steadfast, immovable, always abounding in the work of the Lord, *knowing that in the Lord your labour is not*

---

11. 1 Corinthians 15:26.
12. Romans 6:10-12.

in vain.[13] The resurrection points to eternity future, the goal of our labours in this world. Our efforts at witnessing and discipling will echo forever in the world to come. Don't give up! Keep going!

As Puritan John Boys said, 'The resurrection of Christ is the "Amen" of all his promises.'

Prayer:

Father of Life, I praise you for raising your Son. Thank you for displaying your power and confirming so many promises. Would your Spirit drive the implications of the resurrection deeper into my heart, that I may experience more joy, confidence and urgency in my faith than ever before in my life! In the name of the risen Jesus I pray, Amen.

Meditation:

Which of the resurrection's implications above do you most need imprinted deeper on your heart in this season? Why?

---

13. 1 Corinthians 15:58.

Act IV
The Christian Life

Day 17
The God Who Prays: Christ's Intercession

Having died, risen and ascended for you, Jesus continues to pray for you. He is interceding to the Father for you as you read these words. This doctrine is less well known but its implications are powerful. One example: 'Our prayer life stinks most of the time. But what if you heard Jesus praying aloud for you in the next room? Few things would calm us more deeply.'[1] What is Jesus' intercession?

As a missionary in Asia, Andy Woodland described struggling to translate this idea in a local language. Then an indigenous co-translator said, 'Use the phrase *do paarat*. It's a recommendation an influential person brings on behalf of someone else.' Andy's full understanding of this only emerged through what happened some time afterwards:

> My wife, Ellie, and I had been asked to help a friend's daughter experiencing post-natal complications. Ellie found the girl [and her family] in the ward. I stayed outside with the father. Immediately he turned to me and said 'You must tell Ellie to speak to the doctor and *do paarat* on my daughter's behalf. We are just poor people from a minority group … But if you *do paarat* they will give us proper treatment.' Ellie agreed, not knowing if it would make a difference. Thankfully the doctors did listen and the girl recovered quickly. For us it was a humbling illustration of how Jesus comes before the Father on our behalf.[2]

---

1. Dane Ortlund, *Gentle and Lowly: The Heart of Christ for Sinners and Sufferers* (Crossway, 2020), p. 84.

2. Andy Woodland, 'He loves doing "Paarat" for you' (Christian Reader, May/June 1997), p. 44.

In Romans 8:34, Paul speaks of Jesus as the one 'who is at the right hand of God, who indeed is interceding for us.'[3] The word for 'interceding' is from the verb *entygchano* which means to make requests or appeals to one person on behalf of another person. Jesus is praying to the Father for us!

Why does Paul tell us this? The context gives the answer. Romans 8:31-39 is a magnificent cascade of reasons for believers to take strength and comfort and encouragement no matter how tough the going may get. In particular, Paul's argument in verse 34 is that we can be utterly confident of freedom forever from condemnation for sin:

> Who is to condemn? Christ Jesus is the one who died – more than that, who was raised – who is at the right hand of God, who indeed is interceding for us.[4]

Jesus himself, the very One who will be returning to judge the world for sin, is personally petitioning the Father on our behalf. Although his work was completed on the cross, his ongoing prayers are constantly applying to us the benefits of that work.

Notice as well in verse 34 above how Jesus' intercession follows three prior reasons for our confidence: his death, resurrection and ascension. Here, then, if you are a believer, is what Jesus is praying for you right now up in heaven:

> Father, don't judge [insert your name here]. She is no longer guilty! I died for her. Moreover, the fact you raised me back to life proves that you joyfully accepted my sacrifice. On top of that, Father, the fact you have placed me in this position of honour at your right hand in heaven further proves your glad acceptance of my saving work for her. She is free from condemnation.

Another place where Jesus' intercession is mentioned is Hebrews 7:25:

> He is able to save to the uttermost those who draw near to God through him, since he always lives to make intercession for them.[5]

---

3. Romans 8:34.

4. Romans 8:34.

5. Hebrews 7:25.

'To the uttermost' is a translation of the Greek word *panteles* – *pan* meaning 'all'. The point is completeness. There is not one microscopic sin concealed in one miniscule crevice in your heart which Jesus' salvation-applying prayers for you miss. Conversely, there is no towering mountain of guilt in your life too great to be swept away by Jesus' prayers for you. His intercession for you saves 'to the uttermost.'

We all have skeletons in our cupboards. Some are bigger than others. You may have caused someone's death, or ruined someone's life, or done things which will cause you cringing shame for the rest of your days. But whatever the practical consequences or personal scars, you *are* free from your sin. You are forgiven and accepted and embraced by your Father in heaven. A guilt-free life followed by an eternity of bliss stretches before you. Satan would love you to think otherwise. People with toxic unforgiveness towards you may imply otherwise. Your own flawed heart may try to persuade you otherwise. But Jesus Christ Himself is personally upholding you before His Father. You are free.

Part of the context of Hebrews 7:25 is the permanence of Jesus' priesthood for us. The writer references this in verses 21, 24, 27 and 28, as well as in verse 25 itself: '… he *always* lives to make intercession for them.' Your salvation is not a session that will time out, nor a gift with an expiry date. It is *always*. You don't enter a limited grace period following conversion to help get you up on your feet, after which you are on your own. God's saving kindness to you is *always*. If you have been a believer for many decades but with many stumbles in that time – or if you are new to the Christian life and the years ahead seem daunting – Jesus' securing, cross-applying prayers for you have never ceased and will never cease. His intercession for you is *always*.

And remember not only the intercession but also the intercessor. As Puritan Abraham Wright rejoiced, God 'himself hath appointed us such an intercessor to whom he can deny nothing'.[6] Your eternal salvation is as sure as the Father's love for the Son. Your freedom from condemnation is as sure as the Trinity's unity. Be comforted. Be strengthened. Be encouraged!

---

6. Source unknown.

Prayer:

Father, I praise you that alongside this prayer of mine, you receive the prayers for me of your own Son. Thank you for the confidence this gives me for my freedom from condemnation. Thank you that my salvation is 'to the uttermost' – that as Christ applies it to me, none of my sins are too small for his prayers to catch nor too great for his prayers to cover. Thank you that his prayers are over me constantly, moment-by-moment, for the rest of my life. In the name of my loving, faithful Intercessor, Amen.

Meditation:

If a Christian friend said to you 'What's the point of Jesus praying for us?', how would you reply in a couple of sentences? Which aspect of Jesus' intercession is most precious to you? Why?

Day 18
The God Who Speaks: The Word

Having brought us to salvation by the Word,[1] God then equips us for the Christian life ahead by that same Word.[2] It is spiritual rocket-fuel to power us all the way to heaven, transforming our earthly lives on the way. It is a supernatural resource of extraordinary power. Here are five features of the Word of God.[3]

1. The Bible has complete authority

God's people are able to sense this because of the Holy Spirit's conviction. Listen to Paul's explanation of this to the Corinthians:

> We have received ... the Spirit who is from God, that we might understand the things [referring, in context, to written theological truths] freely given us by God. And we impart this in words not taught by human wisdom but taught by the Spirit, interpreting spiritual truths to those who are spiritual. The natural person does not accept the things of the Spirit of God, for they are folly to him ... They are spiritually discerned.[4]

Additional evidence for the Bible's status as the Word of God also includes:

- Its internal consistency across perhaps forty different authors, out of many varied cultures, over several centuries, and

---

1. 2 Timothy 2:8-10.

2. Philippians 2:16.

3. Wayne Grudem lists these features of Scripture in *Systematic Theology: An Introduction to Biblical Doctrine* (IVP, 1994), pp. 73-135.

4. 1 Corinthians 2:12-14.

in three different languages. The Bible's flawless internal consistency is staggering in this light.

- Its unerring historical accuracy
- Its record of the fulfilment of many prophecies made centuries before
- Its influence on human history, unequalled by any book ever written
- Its transformation of hundreds of millions of lives throughout different times and cultures in history, continuing today
- Its unparalleled beauty and profundity as a piece of literature

When we open the Bible, it is easy to assume we are sitting in judgement on it. The opposite is true. 'For the word of God is living and active, sharper than any two-edged sword, piercing to the division of soul and of spirit, of joints and of marrow, and discerning the thoughts and intentions of the heart.'[5] Opening the Scriptures is a serious enterprise: in doing so, we expose our hearts to God's penetrating truth.

Instead of sitting arrogantly over God's Word, we are to sit joyfully, humbly, obediently under it. 'This is the one I esteem: he who is humble and contrite in spirit and trembles at my word.'[6] Praise God for a wonderfully true and trustworthy authority to follow!

2. The Bible has complete inerrancy

Contrary to popular myth and urban legend, the Bible is trustworthy and without error. Those who assume and propagate the fake news that the Bible contains inconsistencies have a vested interest in doing so: if they were to investigate thoroughly and honestly, and discover otherwise, they would have to repent of their lives and hand those lives over to God, which is an impossibility without God's grace.

In my experience, when those who claim the Bible contains mistakes are gently asked for specifics, they usually turn out to be ignorant. And even in those few places where verses might seem problematic at first, credible solutions do exist.

---

5. Hebrews 4:12.

6. Isaiah 66:2 (NIV).

So be assured! You have a God 'who never lies'.[7] He is a God who, because of His nature, finds it 'impossible ... to lie'.[8] His 'decrees are very trustworthy'.[9] 'The word of the Lord proves true.'[10] The Scriptures are God's gift to you of His 'word of truth'.[11] Rejoice and be confident!

3. The Bible has complete clarity

Some parts of the Bible are undeniably harder to comprehend. Even the leader of the apostles admitted as much.[12] And yet God's Word is clear! As the Psalmist rejoices, 'The unfolding of your words gives light; it imparts understanding to the simple.'[13] How can we explain this paradox?

Any lack of clarity is always in the of eye of the beholder, and occurs for several reasons. For example, the reader may be seeking to ascertain something about which God has chosen not to give an answer in the Bible.[14] Another possibility is that the reader may lack sufficient knowledge, either about the content of Scripture itself or about the topic of which Scripture is speaking. For example, archaeological or historical findings sometimes seem not to match with the Bible's account – until subsequent discoveries come to light.

Most commonly however, Scripture can seem unclear because readers lack the moral[15] and spiritual[16] qualities which are more important than intellectual ability for understanding it. 'The natural person does not accept the things of the Spirit of God, for they are folly to him, and he is not able to understand them because they are spiritually discerned.'[17] Even for believers, hard hearts amount to blind eyes.[18]

---

7. Titus 1:2.

8. Hebrews 6:18.

9. Psalm 93:5.

10. 2 Samuel 22:31.

11. 2 Timothy 2:15.

12. 2 Peter 3:15, 16.

13. Psalm 119:130.

14. Deuteronomy 29:29.

15. 2 Corinthians 4:3-6.

16. 1 Corinthians 2:14-16.

17. 1 Corinthians 2:14.

18. Matthew 22:28, 29.

Praise the Great Communicator for a beautifully clear message. Be asking Him for a clean heart and a dependence on His Spirit to keep being able to perceive it.

4. The Bible has complete necessity

God's Word is not an optional extra. It is not a bonus. It is a vital, indispensable necessity.

It is needed for knowledge of the gospel and for salvation: 'You have been born again ... through the living and abiding word of God.'[19]

It is needed for the ongoing spiritual growth and health of believers: 'Like newborn infants, long for the pure spiritual milk [God's Word] that by it, you may grow up into salvation.'[20]

It is needed as 'the sword of the Spirit' required for us 'to stand against the schemes of the devil ... against the spiritual forces of evil.'[21]

To embark on the Christian life with a casual or non-existent relationship with the Bible is like expecting someone to guess the gospel by which they might be saved. It is like expecting your baby to grow while denying them milk. It is like going on a night patrol in Afghanistan with no night-vision googles, no radio and no weapon. Praise God for His provision of the resource we so urgently need.

5. The Bible has complete sufficiency

In God's Word, we are amply provided with all that we need.

The Word is sufficient to save because it is 'the sacred writings which are able to make you wise for salvation through faith in Christ Jesus'.[22]

The Word is sufficient to sanctify because it is 'profitable for teaching, for reproof, for correction and for training in righteousness, that the man of God may be competent, equipped for every good work'.[23]

The Word is sufficient for teaching us all we will ever need to know. 'The secret things belong to the LORD our God, but the things that are revealed belong to us and to our children forever.'[24]

---

19. 1 Peter 1:23.
20. 1 Peter 2:2.
21. Ephesians 6:11-12, 17.
22. 2 Timothy 3:15.
23. 2 Timothy 3:16, 17.
24. Deuteronomy 29:29.

The sufficiency of God's Word can be remembered by the light-hearted child's acronym of BIBLE: Basic Instructions Before Leaving Earth. The Word of God will not contain everything you want, but it does have all the wisdom and revelation you will ever need. Don't be tempted to elevate other sources of wisdom anywhere near to the supreme value of Scripture. You can have joyful, grateful contentment in what God has given you.

Prayer:

Speaking God, thank you for your loving provision to me of your Word. I praise you for that authoritative, inerrant, clear, necessary, sufficient lamp to my feet and light to my path.[25] Help me to be humble in obeying it, faithful in trusting it, diligent in studying it, urgent in holding to it, and content in accepting it. In the name of the incarnate Word, Amen.

Meditation:

Look again at the prayer, which lists five applications of the characteristics of Scripture we've seen. Which of these five applications are you strongest at? And weakest? Why do you think this is?

---

25. Psalm 119:105.

Day 19
The God Who Hears:
Prayer

I once read about a missionary in a remote area, Herbert Jackson, who had a car that would only start with a push. He came up with a cunning plan. Each morning he would persuade the nearby school children to push his car off. Then, as he made his rounds throughout the day, he would park at the top of a nearby hill or else have to leave the engine running. He did this for years. One day a new missionary came out to join him. Jackson proudly started to explain his ingenious system and the other man opened the bonnet and looked inside. Before Jackson had finished speaking, he interrupted him: 'Doctor Jackson, the only problem is this loose cable!'[1] He gave the cable a quick twist, climbed into the car, turned the key, and to Jackson's amazement the engine burst into life. The power had been there all the time. Only a loose connection had kept Jackson from putting it to work.

Some of you reading this might be Jackson. Your Christian walk seems sluggish and burdensome. You rarely sense the Lord's presence or see Him intervene in your life. Your issue is a loose connection: prayer. Prayer is our link to God's limitless might, 'the key' in the words of R. A. Torrey, 'that unlocks all the storehouses of God's infinite grace and power'.[2] It is God's priceless gift to every believer, without which the path of the Christian life would be impossible.

So how does prayer work? Bluntly, prayer makes things happen. 'Ask, and it will be given to you; seek, and you will find; knock, and

---

1. Source unknown.
2. R. A. Torrey, *The Power of Prayer* (Revell, 1924), p. 25.

it will be opened to you' says Jesus.[3] 'You do not have because you do not ask' writes James.[4]

Yet crucially, while prayer makes things happen, it does so not in a way which undermines God's sovereignty. Prayer doesn't take things out of His hands, or twist His arm into doing something He hadn't planned.[5] Moses is clear in the book of Numbers: 'God is not a man that he should lie nor a son of man that he should change his mind.'[6] In John's words, 'If we ask anything *according to his will*, he hears us.'[7]

So another way of saying that 'prayer makes things happen' would be to say that *God* makes things happen, and that prayer is an essential element in how God chooses to do so. God folds our time-bound prayers into His fore-ordained will, in a way that is over our conceptual horizon but nonetheless real. Elizabeth Elliot describes the upshot: 'Prayer lays hold of God's plan and becomes the link between his will and its accomplishment on earth. Amazing things happen and we are given the privilege of being the channels...' In John Piper's words, prayer 'is the splicing of our limp wire with the lightning bolt of heaven'.[8]

So within God's sovereignty, we pray in order to bring things about in our world. However, we pray not merely for personal agendas and greater comfort. **We pray to advance the Kingdom of God**. James says that 'the prayer of *a righteous person* [a person living for God, as opposed to living for themselves] has great power as it is working'.[9] Piper again: 'It is a wartime walkie-talkie for spiritual warfare, not a domestic intercom to increase the comforts of the saints.'[10]

---

3. Luke 11:9.

4. James 4:2.

5. Occasionally, Scripture suggests that God *can* change His mind in response to prayer. This is because the Bible sometimes describes things from a human perspective instead of a divine perspective. That is, it describes what we see rather than the deeper reality *behind* what we see. This is known as phenomenological language – portraying the visible phenomena of a situation instead of the invisible spiritual realities behind that situation. One example is Moses appearing to change God's mind about destroying his people in Exodus 32:9-14.

6. Numbers 23:19.

7. 1 John 5:14.

8. John Piper, *Brothers We Are Not Professionals* (Blimie and Herman, 2013), p. 68.

9. James 5:16.

10. John Piper, *The Pleasures of God* (Multnomah, 1991), p. 226.

When I get home from work in the evening, I sometimes put something my boys will like in my fist, and they have to pry my fingers open one-by-one. (After longer games, my fingers resemble a set of Allen keys.) Once the boys finally get the sweets in my hand, they run off stuffing them into their mouths, laughing with delight.

Sometimes at least, might this describe our prayer lives? Let's beware of only coming to God for the goodies in His hand – the promotion, the pay rise, the parking spot – and then running off with our focus on the gifts instead of the giver. We pray to prosper the Kingdom. This might sometimes happen to include our own desires for our personal lives being met. Sometimes it may mean the opposite, as it did even for the Apostle Paul at times.[11] Either way, 'Seek first the kingdom of God and his righteousness' taught Jesus, 'and all these things [the things our Father knows we need] will be added to you.'[12]

As well as moving the Kingdom forward practically, **a second reason for praying is to exercise faith in God**. I might *say* I'm trusting God. I might *look* like I'm trusting God. I might even *think* I'm trusting God! Here's the test of whether I *really* trust God: when no one else is looking or will ever know, how much do I pray? Heartfelt, instinctive prayer reassures me that my faith is real. And expressing my faith in prayer will have several effects on me.

- Prayer will grow my faith. Faith is like a muscle: the more it is exercised, the more it develops. Prayer is the gym of faith. Seeds of unbelief will always lurk in our fallen hearts to some degree. Therefore whenever we pray, we implicitly cry with the father in Mark 9:24, 'I believe; help my unbelief!'

- Prayer will increase my peace. As I take stressful burdens from my own shoulders, and honour God by placing them in His hands, I will know more and more of 'the peace of God which surpasses all understanding'.[13]

- Prayer will honour my Father. This is the ultimate point of my existence. We honour our Father when we come to Him,

---

11. 2 Corinthians 12:7-9.

12. Matthew 6:33.

13. Philippians 4:7.

praising Him and acknowledging our dependence on Him by asking Him for things.

A third reason for praying is to experience fellowship with God. Prayer isn't leveraging an impersonal force, but talking to a personal force. It's not a box we tick but a relationship we experience. The Psalmist writes 'The Lord is near to all who call on him.'[14] Therefore, if I'm not in the habit of calling on my Father, I shouldn't be surprised if I don't feel close to Him. The more I make time to talk with Him, the more intimate and fulfilling will be my relationship with Him. That's just how relationships work. To go through your day knowing that the Lord is by your side, listening carefully and lovingly to every syllable you utter to Him, is a wonderful feeling. Especially on tough days.

What a beautiful gift prayer is, from a kind and loving Father! Keep open lines of communication with heaven today. Expect the privilege of a role in moving the Kingdom forward. Anticipate the expansion of your own assurance, faith and peace. Enjoy a sense of intimacy with your Lord.

Prayer:

Listening Father, thank you for the privilege of prayer. Strengthen me with the discipline to persevere with it, but also grant me joy as I commune with you. Thank you that my prayers matter to you, that you take pleasure in them. Glorify yourself by showing me some amazing answers to them. In the name of the One by whom I can speak to you, Amen.

Meditation:

Are there any wrong assumptions or unhelpful patterns of thinking holding back your prayer life? Which of the benefits of prayer outlined here do you feel in most need of?

---

14. Psalm 145:18.

Day 20
The God Who Gathers: Church

Years ago, a friend of mine joined a waiting list to gain admittance to one of the most exclusive clubs in the world. Decades went by and eventually, by proving his credentials and paying enormous fees, he was able to join. The privileges of this club are extraordinary. To an extent they define him. Membership has changed his life.

If you are a believer, my friend has nothing on you. His membership is a piddling, trivial affair compared to yours. You are part of the most privileged group in history. No amount of waiting or paying or proving credentials can gain entry because your membership is by invitation only. The privileges you have entered into exceed anything this world can offer. And they continue for eternity. Welcome to the Church.

A key aid station on the marathon of the Christian life is when God grants a new believer membership in His people. As well as receiving the intercession of His Son (Day 17), setting before you His Word (Day 18) and granting you His privilege of prayer (Day 19), your Father admits you to the company of His saints.

The term for 'church' is *ekklesia* in the New Testament, which literally means 'assembly'. It's a word which can refer to the totality of God's people around the world and across history. But it can also describe any particular, local, visible congregation. Our membership in the global 'Church' implies and requires our membership of a local, healthy 'church', as Scripture bears out.[1]

---

1. Acts 2:42; Ephesians 4:11-13, 16; Hebrews 10:25.

But, to be honest, local church membership is not always easy! After all, churches are collections of sinners. (What could possibly go wrong?) The truth is that there is no perfect church out there. If you ever found one, you would spoil it by joining it. At its most healthy, a local church is a tantalising taste of heaven. But even when a church is far below this ideal, God sovereignly uses the flaws for our good, painful though that may be. Persevering with active service in a local church, through the hard times as well as the easy, is vital for our blessing and growth. It also brings Jesus the glory He deserves.

Consider some of the Bible's many metaphors for the extraordinary, beautiful, sacred, sometimes exasperating phenomenon of the church, and you'll see why God lovingly calls for your maximum commitment. Church is …

The family of God
'I will be a Father to you, and you shall be sons and daughters to me, says the Lord Almighty.'[2] Jesus taught that your gain of the family of God far outweighs the cost of anything you left to follow Him, even before taking eternity into account.[3] Church is the place to receive the practical love and care of the truest family you will ever have.[4] It is also the place to grow through dispensing the same love and care to your sacred siblings. Their older brother sees and will joyfully reward you on the last day, for in ministering to them you were really ministering to Him.[5] Don't hold back from your family!

The house of God
'We are his house'[6] with Jesus as the builder.[7] We are 'living stones … being built up as a spiritual house' with Jesus as 'a cornerstone chosen and precious'.[8] As you meet as a church, contemplate the invisible reality that God Himself is among you. Although some of Sunday's

---

2. 2 Corinthians 6:18.
3. Mark 10:29, 30.
4. Mark 3:31-35.
5. Matthew 25:34-40.
6. Hebrews 3:6.
7. Hebrews 3:3.
8. 1 Peter 2:5, 6.

events may seem unremarkable or mundane on the surface, be awed and humbled by the miraculous reality going on underneath. You're not just setting out chairs or singing songs or listening to a sermon or serving coffee. You're hosting your Creator.

The 'pillar and buttress of the truth'[9]

So says Paul when urging Timothy and his potentially wavering church to stay strong. The next time you're in church and the pastor walks up to preach, reflect on the fact that while God's truth is under intense pressure in our world, you are part of His means of publicly upholding that truth. You get to man the impregnable ramparts He has appointed for the defence of the truth, even as the assault of this world rages against it. Don't desert your post. Feel the duty. Feel the privilege. Look forward to the vindication.

The bride of Christ

Paul pictures this to the Corinthians: 'I betrothed you to one husband, to present you as a pure virgin to Christ.'[10] John writes similarly, 'I saw the holy city, new Jerusalem, coming down out of heaven from God, prepared as a bride adorned for her husband.'[11] In these and other places, one of the points of the metaphor is the church's purity and holiness – the fact that we are 'adorned'. We have been made beautiful by the love of our husband-to-be. Rejoice and let that truth give you impetus to fight sin. Caving in to temptation is acting out of character and wallowing in vile muck. Resisting temptation is acting in character with Jesus' dazzlingly beautiful bride, of which you are a part.

The body of Christ

'You are the body of Christ and individually members of it.'[12] In context, Paul's point is that the members of a church are interdependent, like the different parts of a human body. God has given each of us different but equally valid gifts. We therefore need each other. More than that, Paul

---

9. 1 Timothy 3:15.
10. 2 Corinthians 11:2.
11. Revelation 21:2.
12. 1 Corinthians 12:27.

is clear that we even belong to each other![13] Don't neglect to fill your God-ordained place in the divine mosaic. Don't miss the satisfaction of playing your part in the divine symphony. Don't forgo the fulfilment of fitting beautifully into something bigger than yourself. You are a part in the body of Jesus!

There is also a different sense in which we are the body of Christ: '[God] put all things under [Jesus'] feet and gave him as head over all things to the church, which is his body ...'[14] Here and elsewhere,[15] we are the body *as distinct from* the head which is Christ. Where this metaphor is used, the point is Jesus' glorious authority over all powers that would harm us. As you take your place in the church, you come under the spiritual safety of your King's supreme and sovereign leadership. Assuming that your heart is right, and that your church involvement isn't an empty gesture, your entrance into the church is your entrance into the cosmic air raid shelter which will protect you from Satan and demons.

The Bible's pictures for us abound. There is not space here to examine how the church is like vine branches connected to Christ the vine, through whom we experience fruitfulness;[16] of how it is like an olive tree, a symbol of beauty, vitality and prosperity;[17] of how it is like a flock of sheep, under the powerful, compassionate care of the Chief Shepherd;[18] of how it is like a field of crops, a place of human workers but supernatural growth;[19] of how it is like a royal priesthood, in which its members experience the privilege of representing God to the lost around them;[20] of how it is like other things besides.

Membership in God's people, and involvement in a healthy local outpost of that people is one of the highest privileges of the Christian life. It is essential for honouring God, blessing others and continuing

13. Romans 12:4, 5.
14. Ephesians 1:22, 23.
15. Colossians 2:19.
16. John 15:1-8.
17. Romans 11:17; Jeremiah 11:16; Psalm 52:8.
18. 1 Peter 5:2-4.
19. 1 Corinthians 3:6-9.
20. 1 Peter 2:9.

to grow personally. It is vital to help you and the believers around you keep moving forward towards heaven. Church is God's plan for you. Lean in!

Prayer:

Heavenly Father, I praise you for the church. Thank you for Scripture's pictures of its multi-faceted power and beauty. Help me to be established in a faithful church, not as a consumer but as a contributor. Would this bring about your glory, the good of those around me, and my own blessing. Where church is hard, would I be refined by it, as I persevere with humility and godliness. Where church is easy, would I take deep pleasure in it. In the name of the One who died to assemble the church, Amen.

Meditation:

Of these metaphors for the church, which does your heart most need in this season? Why?

Day 21
The God Who Grows: Sanctification

One essential component of the Christian life is ongoing spiritual growth. 'We ask and urge you in the Lord Jesus, that as you received from us how you ought to walk and to please God, ... you do so *more and more* ... For this is the will of God, your sanctification.'[1]

This sanctification is a gift of God, but one with which we are called to co-operate. 'Work out your own salvation with fear and trembling, for it is God who works in you ...'[2] It requires our own spiritual sweat. Speaking of sanctification, Peter urges 'Make every effort ...'[3]

And sanctification is not a 'nice-to-have'. 'Strive ... for the holiness without which no one will see the Lord' warns the writer to the Hebrews.[4] The choice we face as believers, to put it starkly, is growth or death. That may sound extreme, but that principle often operates in our world. If your newborn baby refuses to grow, he will end up in an Intensive Care Unit while doctors frantically try to figure out what is wrong before it is too late. If crops fail to grow, we conclude that they are dead. So spiritual growth is an authenticating mark of whether we have spiritual life. To be clear, growth doesn't *cause* life – we're saved by faith, not by growth. But growth does *indicate* life. Growth exposes whether the faith we may think we have is genuine or self-delusional.

---

1. 1 Thessalonians 4:1-3.

2. Philippians 2:12, 13.

3. 2 Peter 1:5.

4. Hebrews 12:14.

What does such growth look like in practice? Peter lists some examples:

'Make every effort to *supplement* [notice the idea of growth] your faith with virtue ...' he begins.[5] This is about practical goodness. You do the washing up when it's not your turn. You turn the other cheek when a colleague snaps at you.

'... and virtue with knowledge' Peter goes on.[6] You study the Scriptures daily. You often have a good Christian book on the go. You subscribe to a Christian podcast of sound teaching.

'... and knowledge with self-control ...'[7] Some juicy gossip comes to mind when you're relaxing with a friend, but your conscience pricks you just in time and you manage to hold it in.

'... and self-control with steadfastness ...'[8] Life hits you with a painful blow – unemployment, bereavement, a frightening diagnosis. But you cry out to God and He answers your prayer with strength to keep going for Him. You are steadfast.

'... and steadfastness with godliness ...'[9] The Greek word there for 'godliness' is *eusebeia* which means 'devoutness, piety, devotion to God'. When you wake in the morning, the first object you reach for isn't your phone but your Bible.

'... and godliness with brotherly affection ...'[10] Take that person in your small group at church who unfailingly gets up your nose. You prayerfully commit not only to loving them but even to working hard at *liking* them! You consider what they're dealing with in life which might be making them harder to get on with; you think about their good qualities; you go out of your way to be warm and kind to them.

---

5. 2 Peter 1:5.

6. 2 Peter 1:5.

7. 2 Peter 1:6.

8. 2 Peter 1:6.

9. 2 Peter 1:6.

10. 2 Peter 1:7.

'... and brotherly affection with love.'[11] You lay down your life for your brothers and sisters in practical ways. 'You need a ride? I'll be there.' 'You're short this month? Here's some cash.' 'You're discouraged? I'm taking you out for coffee.'

'Therefore, brothers,' Peter concludes, 'be all the more diligent to confirm your calling and election.'[12]

The story is told of an eagle looking for prey. Before long it spots the carcass of a lamb drifting down a river on an ice-float. It swoops down and starts devouring the meat. Within a few minutes it hears the roar of a gigantic waterfall and sees spray in the distance. 'Just a few more minutes and then I'll fly to safety' it thinks. The waterfall gets closer. 'Just a few more seconds and then I'll fly to safety.' Finally, as the ice-float reaches the waterfall and slowly starts to tip over edge before plunging hundreds of feet to the bottom, the eagle confidently pumps its powerful wings. It knows that just two beats will launch it high into the air. Nothing happens. It starts flapping frantically but still fails to lift. Its claws have frozen into the ice.

Peter writes, 'If you practice these qualities you will never *fall*.'[13] As believers, we have been given wings to get to heaven. When it comes to salvation, 'use them or lose them' doesn't quite apply because true believers can't lose their salvation. But the truth isn't far off. We might say something like 'use them or you may discover one day that you never truly had them, at least not ones that worked'. Peter continues, 'For in this way [of practising these qualities], there will be richly provided for you an entrance into the eternal kingdom of our Lord and Savior Jesus Christ.'[14]

But diligently spreading the wings of sanctification has more functions than authenticating our salvation and strengthening our assurance:[15]

---

11. 2 Peter 1:7.

12. 2 Peter 1:10.

13. 2 Peter 1:10.

14. 2 Peter 1:11.

15. Wayne Grudem lays out some of these functions in *Systematic Theology: An Introduction to Biblical Doctrine* (Inter-varsity Press, 1994), pp. 757, 758.

- It pleases our Father. 'This is the will of God, your sanctification.'[16]

- It tends to bring God's blessing upon us. 'Whoever desires to love life and see good days, let him ... turn away from evil and do good.'[17]

- It spares us God's discipline. 'He disciplines us for our good, that we may share his holiness ... All discipline seems painful rather than pleasant, but later it yields the peaceful fruit of righteousness to those who have been trained by it.'[18]

- It gives God's watching angels joy: 'There is rejoicing in the presence of the angels of God over one sinner who repents.'[19]

- It brings us peace. 'What you have learned and received and heard and seen in me – practice these things, and the God of peace will be with you.'[20]

- It gains us greater rewards in eternity to come. As Jesus will say at the end of time to those who strove for greater obedience, 'Well done, good and faithful servant! Because you have been faithful in a very little, you shall have authority over ten cities.'[21]

- It maintains a clean conscience. Paul knew this: 'I always take pains to have a clear conscience before God and men.'[22] Sanctification enables us to take such pains.

- It heightens our effectiveness for the Kingdom. 'If anyone cleanses himself from what is dishonourable, he will be a vessel for honourable use ... useful to the master of the house, ready for every good work.'[23]

---

16. 1 Thessalonians 4:1-3.
17. 1 Peter 3:10, 11.
18. Hebrews 12:10, 11.
19. Luke 15:10 (NIV).
20. Philippians 4:9.
21. Luke 19:17.
22. Acts 24:16.
23. 2 Timothy 2:21.

- It helps draw the lost towards salvation. 'Let your light shine before others, so that they may see your good works and give glory to your Father who is in heaven.'[24]

What a privilege is sanctification! Be leaning on God's grace today to pursue personal growth. Use your wings!

Prayer:

Patient Father, thank you for your grace in Jesus Christ which is 'training us to renounce ungodliness and worldly passions, and to live self-controlled, upright, and godly lives in the present age'.[25] Keep my focus on my Lord, that I may keep growing in His likeness. Help me to be diligent in pursuing greater spiritual maturity day by day. In the name of the One who though He was sinless, was nonetheless made 'perfect through suffering',[26] Amen.

Meditation:

In which seasons of your life in the past have you experienced the most spiritual growth? Why do you think that was?

---

24. Matthew 5:16.
25. Titus 2:12.
26. Hebrews 2:10.

Day 22
The God Who Trains:
Spiritual Disciplines

In *The Silver Chair* by C. S. Lewis, Jill is about to be sent to Narnia by the lion Aslan. She is on a mission to find a lost prince who was abducted many years earlier. To help Jill, Aslan gives her four signs which will guide her in the quest. He describes them to her in turn.

> As the lion seemed to have finished, Jill thought she should say something. So she said, 'Thank you very much. I see.' 'Child' said Aslan, in a gentler voice than he had yet used, 'perhaps you do not see quite as well as you think. But the first step is to remember. Repeat to me, in order, the four signs.' Jill tried, and didn't get them quite right. So the lion corrected her, and made her repeat them again and again till she could say them perfectly. He was very patient over this.[1]

Then the time comes for Aslan to send Jill. He will do so by blowing her from a cliff top. They start to walk towards the edge.

> Long before she had got anywhere near the edge, the voice behind her said, 'Stand still. In a moment I will blow. But first, remember, remember, remember the signs. ... Whatever strange things may happen to you, let nothing turn your mind from following the signs. And secondly, I give you a warning. Here on the mountain I have spoken to you clearly: I will not often do so down in Narnia. Here on the mountain, the air is clear and your mind is clear; as you drop down into Narnia, the air will thicken. Take great care that it does not confuse your mind. And the signs which you have learned here will not look at all as you expect them to look, when you meet them

---

1. C. S. Lewis, *The Silver Chair* (HarperCollins: 1994), p. 24.

there. That is why it is so important to know them by heart and pay no attention to appearances. Remember the signs and believe the signs. Nothing else matters. And now daughter of Eve, farewell.'[2]

We all have moments of being on the mountain – times when, as Aslan would say, the air is clear and our minds are clear. Decisions in life which would honour God seem easier to see. We have clarity and confidence regarding what faithfulness to Jesus looks like. These times might be during a good sermon, or while we're in a church small group, or discussing spiritual things with good Christian friends. Then afterwards we drop down into the hustle and bustle of life. The air thickens and our minds get confused. Life's stress and busyness and temptations crowd in. Things don't look quite as we thought they would look when we were listening to the sermon or fellowshipping.

Aslan's signs for Jill are like spiritual disciplines. They are behavioural patterns which Scripture urges us to be in the habit of repeating, so they can become second nature to us and keep us on track when the air thickens. Spiritual disciplines are regular, practical habits of devotion which increasingly become a part of our character. They help us stay on the right path despite life's pressures and distractions. We can think of them as the diet and training regime of the spiritual athlete. As Paul writes to Timothy,

> Train yourself for godliness; for while bodily training is of some value, godliness is of value in every way, as it holds promise for the present life and also for the life to come … To this end we toil and strive …[3]

But here we should note a danger. This becomes clear when we read Don Whitney's helpful distinction between being and doing:

> The goal of practicing any given discipline is not about doing as much as it is about being: being like Jesus, being with Jesus. But the biblical way to grow in being more like Jesus is through the rightly motivated doing of the biblical, spiritual disciplines.[4]

Here is the danger: doing without being equals legalism. We are saved by faith and not by works. Focusing exclusively on our disciplines

---

2. C. S. Lewis, *The Silver Chair* (HarperCollins: 1994), pp. 25, 26.

3. 1 Timothy 4:7, 8, 10.

4. Don Whitney – https://www.desiringgod.org/interviews/what-are-spiritual-disciplines   Accessed November 2021.

instead of our hearts is spiritually fatal. Jesus exposed this in the worst legalists of His own day:

> You Pharisees cleanse the outside of the cup and of the dish, but inside you are full of greed and wickedness. You fools! Did not he who made the outside make the inside also? But give as alms those things that are within.[5]

In that last sentence, Jesus is saying 'Your doing must flow from your being.' Doing is worse than pointless if it does not come from grace-transformed, God-honouring being. Paul's rousing command to Timothy above, about training oneself for godliness, continues, crucially, with these words: 'To this end we toil and strive [note the doing], *because we have our hope set on the living God.*'[6] Our doing must follow from our being.

But while doing without being equals empty legalism, being without doing equals dead orthodoxy. 'What good is it, my brothers, if someone says he has faith but does not have works? Can that faith save him?'[7] Implied answer: No! And so God in His goodness lays down spiritual disciplines as opportunities to live out our faith. These are avenues for our God-granted being to overflow in God-honouring doing. If approached in this way, the pursuit of spiritual disciplines glorifies Him, blesses others, authenticates our salvation and strengthens our faith.

In this light, we can think of the following as spiritual disciplines:

- Studying Scripture
- Praying
- Giving
- Fasting
- Fellowshipping
- Confessing
- Worshipping
- Resting
- Celebrating

---

5. Luke 11:39, 40.

6. 1 Timothy 4:10.

7. James 2:14.

- Serving
- Witnessing
- Discipling

We could mention more activities, but the principle is simple: these are specific, repetitive actions presented in the Bible as worth pursuing with diligence and determination, so that they increasingly become part of us. They are worth planning for in advance. They are worth making sacrifices for. In other words, they are worth being disciplined.

Maybe as you've read these words today, the air has felt clear and your mind has felt clear. You know that pursuing spiritual disciplines makes sense. You know they are priceless opportunities for life-changing growth. If so, there will be times in the coming days when you drop down and the air thickens. Resolve now to live out your faith in some of the Bible's ways listed above. Make specific plans to safeguard their regular practice in your life. Commit to keep going back, no matter what, to the spiritual gym. Ask God for strength and joy and perseverance and progress as you engage with spiritual disciplines. And most importantly of all, cry out to God for a heart from which they will come naturally, as overflowing manifestations of His saving grace.

Prayer:

God of grace, I praise you for your provision of spiritual disciplines. Thank you for these ways for living out and developing my faith. Thank you for the assurance they give me, the blessing they give others, and the glory they give you. And thank you for your power, through spiritual disciplines, to strengthen me for persevering in the Christian life. Guard me from the temptation of seeking to be justified through them, or allowing them to become empty, legalistic actions while my heart quietly drifts from you. Use them for great good in my life. In the name of the One who disciplined Himself, setting His face 'like flint'[8] to go to the cross, Amen.

Meditation:

Of the spiritual disciplines listed above, which are you in most need of right now? Why? What might be practical ways of embedding them deeper in your life in this season?

---

8. Isaiah 50:7; Luke 9:51

Day 23
The God Who Mobilises: Ministry

Picture the scene. You have been into the local recruiting office and signed up to serve in the army. You have undergone months of basic training. You have been assigned to a unit and undergone further months of specialist training. And now here you sit, far from home in a sweltering Portakabin, uniformed, armed, and about to go on patrol in an operational theatre for the very first time. The platoon commander is issuing the patrol orders, pointing out locations on the map-board and running through vital information one last time. As he concludes and everyone gets up to go, you reflect on the fact that the last year has all been leading up to this moment. You are finally about to fulfil the reason for which the army has invested so much in you, the reason for which you joined. You congratulate yourself on the journey you have taken to become a soldier. As the others file out to go on patrol, you quietly sneak back to your sleeping quarters, hang up your kit, fix yourself a coffee, climb into your sleeping bag, and start relaxing with a movie on your laptop.

As with previous topics like sanctification (Day 21) and spiritual disciplines (Day 22), engaging in ministry isn't an optional extra for believers who are so inclined. It is the very mission *for which* we have been saved. Paul doesn't tell Timothy to think about the good fight, or to train for the good fight, or even to cheer for the right side in the good fight! '*Fight* the good fight!' he pleads.[1]

And in fact, the stakes couldn't be higher: being active in ministry is an authenticating mark of a person who is truly saved. Paul's

---

1. 1 Timothy 6:12.

injunction to Timothy continues, 'Fight the good fight of the faith. *Take hold of the eternal life to which you were called ...*'[2] In Jesus' parable of the minas,[3] the words of the master to the servant who defiantly did nothing are unequivocal and devasting. Exactly the same is true in His similar parable of the talents.[4] The military recruit who signs up and proudly wears the uniform but refuses to soldier when the time comes doesn't remain in the army for long.

So what is ministry? Ministry is defined by Paul as 'building up the body of Christ'.[5] Ministry is 'ministering' to others. It means putting into practice the spiritual gifts God has given every believer for this very purpose: 'As each has received a gift, use it to serve one another, as good stewards of God's varied grace.'[6] Ministry means being willingly mobilised by the Lord for His purposes in our world.

It can be tempting to think of ministry as something pastors and church staff teams and other leaders do for us, while we observe and receive. In this picture, we are in the stands at a sporting event, and they are the professional players performing feats before us. The reality is very different. They are the coaches and the water carriers and the medics, and *we* are the ones on the pitch. Paul describes it to the Ephesians in this way: 'And he gave the apostles, the prophets, the evangelists, the pastors and teachers *to equip the saints* [all believers] *for the work of ministry.*'[7] You were saved to serve. 'We are his workmanship, created in Christ Jesus *for good works* which God prepared beforehand, that we should walk in them.'[8]

Here are some other things Scripture tells us about ministry:

- **You have been equipped for ministry.** 'As each has received a gift [a specific ability from God], *use it to serve one another.*'[9]

- **You have been authorised for ministry.** In the words of the risen Jesus: 'All authority in heaven and on earth has

2. 1 Timothy 6:12.

3. Luke 19:11.

4. Matthew 25:14.

5. Ephesians 4:12.

6. 1 Peter 4:10.

7. Ephesians 4:11.

8. Ephesians 2:10.

9. 1 Peter 4:10.

been given to me. *Go, therefore*, and make disciples of all nations ...'[10]

- **You have been given the standard for ministry.** In the section in Ephesians where Paul discusses ministry, he begins, 'I ... urge you to walk [that is, to be active, to do ministry] in a manner worthy of the calling to which you have been called.'[11] We don't do ministry casually or carelessly or half-heartedly. We do it in a way that reflects the magnificent, eternal salvation to which we have been called. It is sacred.

- **You have been given the example for ministry.** After getting down on His knees to wash His disciples' feet, Christ says these words: 'I have given you an example, that you also should do just as I have done to you.'[12] This breath-taking display of sacrificial, practical, servant-hearted humility is the fundamental paradigm for all of our ministry.

- **You have been given brothers and sisters who need your ministry.** We are all different parts of the body of Christ with different functions, and Paul explains, 'The eye cannot say to the hand, "I have no need of you," nor again the head to the feet, "I have no need of you."'[13] Your own spiritual family members need you. From my experience of human nature and of church, they need you probably far more than either you or they realise!

- **You are responsible and accountable for your ministry.** In Matthew 25 and Luke 19, Jesus tells similar parables which make the same point: one day our Master will hold each of us personally accountable for what we did or didn't do with the gifts He gave us.[14] More than this, the parables make clear that we will experience eternal consequences, both positive and negative.

---

10. Matthew 28:18, 19.

11. Ephesians 4:1.

12. John 13:15.

13. 1 Corinthians 12:21.

14. Matthew 25:14-30; Luke 19:11-27.

- **You will be rewarded for your ministry.** Here are words which, if we hear them from the Lord one day, will mean more to us than all the accolades and achievements of this world: 'Well done, good and faithful servant. You have been faithful over a little; I will set you over much. Enter into the joy of your master.'[15] [16]

Take courage and confidence from these certainties! Ministry isn't always easy but giving it our best is always right. As Paul exhorts Timothy: 'Always be sober-minded, endure suffering, do the work of an evangelist, *fulfil your ministry.*'[17] Paul continues,

> I have fought the good fight, I have finished the race, I have kept the faith. Henceforth there is laid up for me the crown of righteousness, which the Lord, the righteous judge, will award to me on that day, and not only to me but also to all who have loved his appearing.[18]

Keep fighting. Keep running. Keep serving those around you, and through them the Lord Himself. 'The King will answer them, "Truly I say to you, as you did it to one of the least of these my brothers, you did it to me."'[19] Having been set up for ministry in the many significant ways outlined above, don't now slink back to your sleeping quarters, hang up your kit and watch movies. Head out on patrol. The battle is the Lord's. Despite our struggles, overall victory is assured. Seek out and embrace the active role which God has prepared for you on the winning side!

Prayer:

Father, thank you for the honour of ministry. Thank you for this privilege of serving, this opportunity for evidencing my salvation, this mission for which you saved me. Help me to jump in with both feet. Make clear the spiritual gifts you've given me, and give me opportunities and the heart to exercise them for the blessing of

---

15. Matthew 25:21.
16. See Day 30 for the idea of privileged responsibilities in the New Creation.
17. 2 Timothy 4:5.
18. 2 Timothy 4:7-8.
19. Matthew 25:40.

others. Give me energy and fulfilment and joy as I do so. Mobilise me I pray. In the name of the greatest servant of all, who ministered to me on the cross and ministers to me still, Amen.

Meditation:

What serving needs are you aware of in your church or in the lives of believers around you? Regardless of what you think your gifts are, what would it take practically for you to start ministering in these ways?

Day 24
The God Who Refines: Suffering

The insect bite, the upset stomach, the frustration at work, the aching loneliness, the relentless debt, the tumultuous marriage, the devastating bereavement, the crushing depression – we live in a world of pain. Like the telescreens in Orwell's *1984*, its volume in our lives can vary from high to low, but never quite be fully muted.

And as hard as this may be to hear at times, your suffering is happening according to your sovereign Father's good purposes. We thought about this at length on Day 5, 'The God Who Arranges: Providence'. Your pain has purpose. Every last throb of it. 'For those who love God, all things work together for good ...'[1] You are not being pitched about according to the whim of a pitiless universe. You are being handled according to the wisdom of a loving Father. Your suffering is not random. It has beautiful, profound significance. Scottish Puritan Samuel Rutherford knew this when he wrote to a friend, 'I would wish each cross were looked in the face seven times, and were read over and over again. It is the messenger of the Lord, and speaks something.'[2] Today we consider three of the many divine purposes behind your pain.

1. To discipline and refine us

The Lord disciplines the one he loves, and chastises every son whom he receives. ... He disciplines us for our good, that we may share His

---

1. Romans 8:28.

2. Samuel Rutherford, *The Loveliness of Christ* ed. Helen Lister (Banner of Truth, 2007), p. 42.

holiness. For the moment all discipline seems painful rather than pleasant, but later it yields the peaceful fruit of righteousness to those who have been trained by it.[3]

In *The Horse and His Boy* by C. S. Lewis, Aravis is fleeing Calormen for Archenland when she is attacked by a lion. It starts to maul her but then abruptly departs. We learn later that the lion was in fact Aslan, the central Christ figure in Lewis' Narnia series. When she discovers this, Aravis cannot help wonder why the good Aslan would have hurt her so badly. He reveals that her wounds corresponded exactly to the flogging she had earlier brought upon a slave. He explains to her,

> The scratches on your back, tear for tear, throb for throb, blood for blood, were equal to the stripes laid on the back of your stepmother's slave because of the drugged sleep you cast upon her. You needed to know what it felt like.[4]

Until now, the privileged Aravis had been too arrogant to care what happened to the girl. She had been contemptuous of those beneath her station. Now she has been given an insight into the lives of others. Now she is made more humble and compassionate. Now her heart is softened. Often we may not see how or why we are being disciplined. But our kind and loving King knows what He is doing.

2. To turn our self-reliance into God-reliance

> For we do not want you to be unaware, brothers, of the affliction we experienced in Asia … Indeed, we felt that we had received the sentence of death. But that was to make us rely not on ourselves but on God who raises the dead.[5]

Our sufferings are sometimes the nerve endings which stop us from inadvertently destroying ourselves. They prevent us from running over the cliff-edge of our self-reliance. They guard us from the fatal delusion to which we are instinctively prone, that we *are* God and so don't really *need* God.

---

3. Hebrews 12:6, 10, 11.

4. C. S. Lewis, *The Horse and His Boy* (HarperCollins: 1994), p. 216.

5. 2 Corinthians 1:8, 9.

For Icarus, this kind of suffering would have been the wax of his wings starting to scald his skin so that he distanced himself from the sun, before it melted completely and they disintegrated. Listen to your suffering carefully. Don't miss the loving, vital warning it may be offering you.

3. To enable our identification with Jesus

Paul cites a function of the pain in his life when defending his authenticity to the Galatians: 'From now on let no one cause me trouble, *for I bear on my body the marks of Jesus*.'[6] His participation in Christ's suffering validates his true identity.

Identifying with Jesus through suffering also puts us in a position to minister to others. Listen to Paul telling the Corinthians that he is 'always carrying in the body the death of Jesus, *so that the life of Jesus may also be manifested in our bodies ...* So death is at work in us, *but life in you*.'[7]

Paul describes another purpose of the pain in his life when he tells the Philippians that he shares in Christ's 'sufferings, becoming like him in his death, *that by any means possible I may attain the resurrection from the dead*'.[8] Paul wants to identify with Jesus fully, all the way, even including His suffering and death, because that is the only path to life.[9]

We are saved because, through repentance and faith, we are *in Christ*. And a key way of identifying with Christ is not only to suffer, but to suffer well. We bear our pain in a God-honouring way, because that is how Jesus bore His. In other words, we meet our suffering with trust in God,[10] patient endurance,[11] an absence of bitter resentment,[12] and a focus on the joy which lies beyond the fleeting pain of this world.[13]

---

6. Galatians 6:17.

7. 2 Corinthians 4:10, 12.

8. Philippians 3:10, 11.

9. Luke 9:23.

10. Luke 22:44.

11. 2 Timothy 2:3.

12. Luke 23:34.

13. Hebrews 12:2.

So when, because of your faith, you are snubbed by friends, cold-shouldered by neighbours, resented by family or gossiped about by colleagues, don't waste this precious opportunity to suffer as your Saviour suffered. When you choose to forego sleep for the sake of time in God's Word, to forgo convenience for the sake of serving in church, to forgo comfort for the sake of witnessing to others, to forgo luxuries for the sake of sacrificial giving, don't squander that precious Father-ordained chance to suffer well! Treasure the reality that in some small way, you are treading Jesus' path.

Ultimately, in these three and other ways, we suffer for God's glory. We suffer well to display the God who is sovereign over our suffering, who wonderfully uses it, who for our sakes experienced it, and who will one day end it. Having been rebuked and beaten by the Jewish council, the apostles leave 'rejoicing that they were *counted worthy to suffer dishonour for the name*'.[14] We suffer well to show that Jesus is worth it.

Earlier we saw that focusing on the eternal joy of which we are on the brink is part of what it means to bear our pain well. But this is also vital for being able to bear it at all. Paul's calculated perspective is that 'the sufferings of this present time are not worth comparing with the glory that is to be revealed to us'.[15] The following words of Samuel Rutherford stopped me in my tracks the first time I read them. I pray they do the same for you.

> When we shall come home ... when our heads shall find the weight of the eternal crown of glory, and when we shall look back to pains and sufferings; then shall we see life and sorrow to be less than one step or stride from a prison to glory; and that our little inch of time – suffering is not worthy of our first night's welcome home to heaven.[16]

Our suffering may sometimes feel like a hindrance in our lives. We may be tempted to think that if it wasn't for the distracting pain holding us back, we could be and do so much more for the Kingdom. The exact opposite is the truth. As Rutherford saw so clearly, 'Christ's

---

14. Acts 5:41.

15. Romans 8:18.

16. Samuel Rutherford, *The Loveliness of Christ* ed. Helen Lister (Banner of Truth, 2007), p. 19.

cross is such a burden as sails are to a ship or wings to a bird.'[17] As you travel the path to heaven through this vale of tears, harness your pain for the sake of your progress.

Prayer:

Loving, kind, wise Father, forgive me for distrusting or resenting or fearing the troubles which according to Scripture you 'bring' into my life and which I receive 'from you'.[18] Thank you for bringing your good out of their evil. Help me, in Rutherford's words, to look each of my crosses in the face seven times, and to read them over, as your messengers. I thank you for the many ways you work through my suffering for your glory and my good. I praise you for the coming eternity, the dazzling brightness of which will far eclipse even the most intense suffering of this brief life. Sustain me. Comfort me. Strengthen me. As I continue my journey home, help me to harness my pain for my progress. In the name of the One who suffered so well for me, Amen.

Meditation:

What is the single greatest source of suffering in your life right now? How do the categories in this chapter help you to interpret it? How can you leverage it?

---

17. Samuel Rutherford, *The Loveliness of Christ* ed. Helen Lister (Banner of Truth, 2007), p. 21.

18. Job 42:11; Job 2:10.

Day 25

The God Who Keeps: Perseverance

As a child on holiday in the Scottish Highlands, I would go for long treks in the mountains with my father. On one occasion we found ourselves trying to cross a fast-flowing river. Wading it was no problem for my dad but I could only just keep my footing in the foaming white water. As I set out from the bank, he positioned himself next to me, just downstream, and shadowed me across, ready to catch me should I be swept off my feet. Although the going wasn't easy, I had absolute confidence that I was safe. My passage to the other side was never in doubt.

As believers, we can say the same. Having rescued us, God securely keeps us. Once saved, always saved. He ensures our perseverance all the way to the finish. As Richard Baxter noted, 'In our first paradise in Eden there was a way to go out but no way to go in again. But as for the heavenly paradise, there was a way to go in, but no way to go out.'[1]

Talking about His sheep, Jesus says, 'they will never perish, and no one will snatch them out of my hand. My Father, who has given them to me, is greater than all, and no one is able to snatch them out of the Father's hand.'[2] When the Devil had the Apostle Simon Peter in his cross hairs, Jesus was able to say: 'Simon, Simon, Satan has asked to sift you as wheat. But I have prayed for you, Simon, that your faith may not fail.'[3] If you are a true believer, Jesus Christ prays for you

---

1. Richard Baxter, *A Puritan Golden Treasury*, compiled by I. D. E. Thomas (Banner of Truth, 2000), p. 91.

2. John 10:28, 29.

3. Luke 22:31 (NIV).

also, to this day (see Day 17). He will not let your faith fail either. And notice Jesus' tender, personal tone to Peter, using his original name three times in two sentences. Christ sustains us not merely as numbers but as precious individuals, known to Him personally. Be secure. Be confident. Be encouraged.

Yet alongside this encouragement that God keeps us, is an urgent and deadly serious exhortation: whatever you do, no matter what, at all costs, regardless of the earthly consequences, keep going! Keep yourself in the faith!

Scripture is unashamed of this apparent paradox. Jude, for example, is able to conclude his letter with 'Now to him who is able to keep you ...' just three verses after writing '... keep yourselves in the love of God ...'[4] The encouragement that God keeps us and the insistent exhortation to keep ourselves come to us hand in hand. So what is going on here? How can Scripture insist on both simultaneously? God keeps you. Keep yourself. Which is it?

The answer is seen when we realise how the Bible often links the two. The encouragement flows from the exhortation. For example, Paul writes to the Philippians, 'Work out your own salvation with fear and trembling [keep yourself!] *for* it is God who works in you [God keeps you!] ...'[5] He writes to the Corinthians, 'Thanks be to God, who gives us the victory through our Lord Jesus Christ. [God keeps you!] *Therefore*, my beloved brothers, be steadfast, immoveable [keep yourself!] ...'[6]

Because of the encouragement, therefore the exhortation. God never lets true believers go. So show yourself a true believer by keeping going! The writer to the Hebrews makes this point urgently to his readers:

> Take care, brothers, lest there be in any of you an evil, unbelieving heart, leading you to fall away from the living God. But exhort one another every day, as long as it is called 'today', that none of you may be hardened by the deceitfulness of sin. For we have come to share in Christ, if indeed we hold our original confidence firm to the end.[7]

---

4. Jude 21, 24.
5. Philippians 2:12, 13.
6. 1 Corinthians 15:57, 58.
7. Hebrews 3:12-14.

Such warning notes are given not to paralyse us but to propel us. They drive us to the daily faithfulness to Christ in which we experience the wonderful assurance of eternal security. They encourage in us the commitment to Jesus by which we see reassuring evidence of His unbreakable hold on us.

'Once saved, always saved' is a helpful saying, in line with much of Scripture's teaching – as long as we remember that the sign of whether we really *were* once saved is that we are seeking by God's power to live for Jesus *today*. I knew my dad loved his son and would keep him from being swept down the mountainside. But it was by actually walking with him through the torrent that I showed myself to be that son.

And holding onto both the encouragement and the exhortation is not merely an intellectual, theological game. Having either at the exclusion of the other is disastrous. The encouragement without the exhortation will tend towards complacent licentiousness and cheap grace (which is no grace at all). Conversely, the exhortation without the encouragement will tend towards legalism and spiritual insecurity.

In other words, thinking only 'God will keep me no matter what' will make me vulnerable to abusing that truth as a blank cheque for godless living. Conversely, thinking only 'I must keep myself' will leave me assuming salvation depends on my ability to walk closely with the Lord, and therefore frantically manufacturing external actions.

Whereas, it is precisely our conviction that God infallibly guards His children that motivates us to live in a way that shows us to be truly His children. Jonathan Edwards appreciated the connection between the two when he wrote, 'They that will not live godly lives find out for themselves that they are not elected; they that will live godly lives have found out for themselves that they are elected.'[8]

As I write these words, I can feel the stiffness and the aches of a forty-year-old body in training for an upcoming marathon. To say I 'run' flatters my lumbering gait. But I stick at it. Why? Three reasons. Number one, I'm an idiot. As for the second two reasons, I want the health benefits which come daily from the training; and I long for the future fulfilment of my goal. I long to cross that finish line.

---

8. Jonathan Edwards, 'Miscellaneous Remarks Concerning Perseverance of the Saints' in *The Works of Jonathan Edwards*, volume 2, ed. Thomas Schafer (Yale University Press,1994), p. 569.

FROM EVERLASTING TO EVERLASTING

These are the benefits of persevering in the Christian life: the process and the prize. The growth now and the glory then. Paul places these two encouragements side by side as he writes about his own hard slog of perseverance to the Corinthians:

> So we do not lose heart. Though our outer self is wasting away, our inner self is being renewed day by day [the process]. For this light momentary affliction is preparing for us an eternal weight of glory beyond all comparison [the prize] ...[9]

Here's how he describes the same two benefits of his endurance to the Romans:

> Endurance produces character [the process], and character produces hope [the anticipation of the eternal future prize] ...[10]

Perseverance is priceless. It is something to long for urgently. For over twenty years I've been praying, 'Lord, please would I still be living for you five years from now, and twenty years from now, and fifty years from now, if you haven't already taken me home.' That is a good prayer. Let God's sovereign, unbreakable grip on you give rise in your Christian life to this approach of Paul's: '... straining forward to what lies ahead, I press on toward the goal for the prize of the upward call of God in Christ Jesus.'[11]

Prayer:

Heavenly Father, I praise you for the encouragement of your ever-lasting, unbreakable grip of grace. Help me to respond faithfully to your loving exhortation alongside it, and persevere with you at any cost. Keep me going I pray. Grant me the encouragements of the process now, in personal spiritual growth, but also of the prospect of the prize to come. In the name of the One who did not come down off the cross before His mission was complete, but who persevered to the end, Amen.

Meditation:

If you were Satan, what would be the main ways you would tempt someone in your own current position to give up on the Christian life?

---

9. 2 Corinthians 4:16, 17.

10. Romans 5:4.

11. Philippians 3:13, 14.

Day 26

The God Who Accompanies Through the Valley: Death

Our early morning foot patrol into the heart of the city had gone smoothly, and we arrived at the Iraqi police station without incident. As we entered the compound, I posted sentries. These included two guys on the roof to give us early warning of hostile crowds gathering while we were inside. Everything was quiet and calm.

I was sipping coffee with the police chief inside the building when suddenly shouts of 'Man down!' burst over the net. One of the rooftop soldiers had taken a sniper's bullet from across the street. It had entered his cheek and exited the back of his head. He was still breathing but with all the blood in his hair, we struggled to find the exit wound. Within minutes, one of our vehicles screeched to a halt outside the compound to evacuate him. I ran out to it carrying his blood-filled helmet while he was loaded up. I had sat opposite him that morning at breakfast as he cracked jokes and ate boiled eggs (whites only – he was into fitness and in great shape). He took several hours to die. And then just like that, the popular, life-loving twenty-two-year-old was gone forever.

Whomever death snatches, from pre-natal babies and frail old men in hospital beds to fit young men on battlefields, it never fails to shock. Something about it is brutally wrong. Death casts its shadow over our lives and God's Word has much to say about it. Here's a small sample:

First, death is unnatural. It didn't exist when God made this creation and it won't exist when He makes the New Creation. It's not in our 'factory settings'. It's a virus that found a way in later. It sprang up because we rejected God and chose sin. 'Just as sin came into the world through one man, and death through sin … so death spread to all men because all sinned.'[1] The world will soon be free of death but until then, we experience this jarring, temporary, dysfunctional phenomenon.

This means that we mustn't resign ourselves to the apparent victory of death over us. We must fight the temptation of drifting into fear or cynicism or quiet hopelessness. We are more than worm-food. C. S. Lewis expresses this truth powerfully:

> Creatures are not born with desires unless satisfaction for those desires exists. A baby feels hunger: well, there is such a thing as food. A duckling wants to swim: well, there is such a thing as water. Men feel sexual desire: well, there is such a thing as sex. If I find in myself a desire which no experience in this world can satisfy [such as the desire not to die – 'He has put eternity into man's heart'[2]], the most probable explanation is that I was made for another world … I must keep alive in myself the desire for my true country, which I shall not find until after death; I must never let it get snowed under or turned aside; I must make it the main object of life to press on to that country and to help others to do the same.[3]

Second, death is inevitable. As surely as the sun will set on you tonight, you will one day die.[4] The inevitability of death points us to the briefness and fragility of life:

> You return man to dust. … A thousand years in your sight are but as yesterday when it is past, or as a watch in the night … [Human life is] like a dream, like grass that is renewed in the morning: in the morning it flourishes and is renewed; in the evening it fades and withers.[5]

This means we mustn't be naïve about death. In other words, we mustn't cling too tightly to this ephemeral world. According to Peter, we are 'sojourners' – brief visitors just passing through.[6] We must

---

1. Romans 5:12.
2. Ecclesiastes 3:11.
3. C. S. Lewis, *Mere Christianity* (Collins, 2012), p. 137.
4. Ecclesiastes 7:2.
5. Psalm 90:3-6.
6. 1 Peter 2:11.

beware the common, tragic mistake of the rich fool in Jesus' parable.[7] He was devoted to building a great life for himself but never factored in his own death. Because of this, for all his wealth and success, his life was in fact a wasted failure.

Third, Scripture is realistic and honest that death is painful. In Scripture, the death of a friend causes Jesus to weep.[8] It's described as bitter, dark, and the last enemy.[9] We recoil at death for several reasons including: the pain of the physical process, the separation from loved ones, the end of earthly joys and hopes, and the shrouded mystery of what dying actually feels like.

The painfulness of death means that we must allow ourselves to mourn it. The Bible doesn't indulge in denial over the horror and tragedy of death. We don't need to either. Of course Christ has defeated it, of course its sting has been removed, and of course believers will emerge safely out of the other side. But none of that negates the appropriate response of mourning others' deaths or feeling sober about our own. Death is still a curse. Grieving over it is not shameful or weak but healthy and honest. Just ask Jesus at Lazarus' graveside.[10] 'Weep with those who weep' encourages Paul.[11] We're not required to whistle in the dark.

Yet as we mourn, we do not need to 'grieve as others do, who have no hope'[12] because **fourth, death for the believer is impotent.** Death has been defanged. Paul rejoiced,

> 'O death, where is your victory? O death, where is your sting?' The sting of death is sin, and the power of sin is the law. But thanks be to God, who gives us the victory through our Lord Jesus Christ.[13]

The 'sting of death is sin' because sin caused death as well as the damnation to which it leads. Paul's cry of victory is because on the cross, Jesus took our sin and endured our hell. For the believer, death is

---

7. Luke 12:16-21.

8. John 11:35.

9. 1 Corinthians 15:56, 1 Samuel 15:32, Luke 1:79.

10. John 11:35.

11. Romans 12:15.

12. 1 Thessalonians 4:13.

13. 1 Corinthians 15:55-57.

no longer the trapdoor to a terrifying tragedy but the gateway to glory. What is more, the Good Shepherd Himself comes to accompany us safely through it. 'Even though I walk through the valley of the shadow of death … you are with me.'[14] He will meet us in the valley.

This means that alongside appropriate mourning, we can also choose to rejoice in the midst of death. Christian joy is a choice. 'Rejoice in the Lord *always*; again I will say: Rejoice!'[15] Ask God's help in cultivating the ability to say, even through the tears, 'I rejoice that my baby, child, parent, friend, though I miss them to the point of heartbreak, now has more rest and peace and joy than I can imagine.'[16] And cultivate that perspective on your own impending promotion to glory.

Prayer:

God of life, I acknowledge that through the death of Christ you achieved the death of death. Help me to cultivate a healthy, biblical view of death, for the sake of my joy and your glory. When I lose people close to me, help me to grieve well. When the time comes for you to call me home, help me to die well. Thank you that your Son will meet me in the Valley. In the name of the One who conquered death, Jesus Christ, Amen.

Meditation:

How much do you fear death? Why? From this chapter, what would you apply to yourself to bring that fear into line with the truth?

---

14. Psalm 23:4.

15. Philippians 4:4.

16. On the intensely difficult subject of the death of unbelieving loved ones, we must cling to the following truths: 1) God judges fairly and justly (Gen. 18:25); 2) The severity with which He judges someone is according to what they knew, not what they didn't (Luke 12:47, 48); 3) Our happiness in eternity will be unclouded regardless of missing loved ones (Rev. 21:4). This is because the reasons for which we love unbelievers in this life will no longer be true of them in eternity. In this life it was God's grace in them which made them lovable to us, as all good comes from Him (Ps. 16:2). In eternity, they will be cut off from that grace (2 Thess. 1:9). So in one sense at least, from our point of view, they will be different people from those whom we know in this life. They will no longer *be* our loved ones. 4) God takes no pleasure in the death of unbelievers (Ezek. 33:11); 5) Our grief in this world over perishing loved ones is a grief that was shared by Jesus (Luke 19:41-44) and Paul (Rom. 9:1-3) among others in Scripture; 6) Our current grief matters to God. He is the God of all comfort (2 Cor. 1:3-5).

Act V
The Life To Come

Day 27

The God Who Receives: Heaven

As soon as you die, you will find yourself in heaven. But what does that really mean? Will it be better than perching on a cloud in a nightgown and clutching a harp upon which you will plink away for eternity? Ortlund paints a better, more biblical picture: 'One day God is going to walk us through the wardrobe into Narnia, and we will stand there, paralysed with joy, wonder, astonishment, and relief.'[1] Scripture gives us some tantalising glimpses of the reality that awaits us.

Heaven is the place our souls go when we die physically.[2] There we will wait with Christ until the Second Coming before accompanying Him back and being reunited with perfected, resurrected bodies.[3] Here are some of the ways Scripture describes heaven:

First, **heaven is a place of rest**. '"Blessed indeed [are the dead who die in the Lord]," says the Spirit, "that they may rest from their labours."'[4] 'Then they [souls in heaven] were each … told to rest a little longer.'[5] Hebrews 4 repeatedly describes entering God's salvation after this life as entering His rest. Scripture also uses sleep as an analogy for the believer's physical death, partly to communicate the idea of rest.[6]

---

1. Dane Ortlund, *Gentle and Lowly: The Heart of Christ for Sinners and Sufferers* (Crossway, 2020), p. 209.

2. Acts 7:59.

3. 1 Thessalonians 4:14, 16.

4. Revelation 14:13.

5. Revelation 6:11.

6. When the Bible likens dying to going to sleep, that analogy is from the point of view of the living. It is phenomenological language, in other words the language

Such respite will be unlike any you have ever experienced. It will be deeper than human language can describe. Try to imagine total, utter relief for the first time in your life from all sin, anxiety, fatigue, physical pain, mental illness, stress, grief, fear, frustration, opposition and disappointment. In their place will be an overwhelming sense of peace. You will finally, for the first time ever, be truly at rest.

Heaven is also a place of consciousness. Jesus' promise to the thief on the cross wasn't that he would experience oblivion that same day but paradise.[7] The Apostle John describes believers in heaven crying out to God.[8] The pre-death experience of heaven which Paul was given, which he describes to the Corinthians, was vividly conscious.[9]

I've had a general anaesthetic a few times. I've always found the sensation of slipping into unconsciousness unnerving, like gradually sinking into a black fog, even if I'm confident I'll wake from it later. That's not a picture of entering heaven for the believer. If anything, leaving this world for heaven will be like *exiting* a fog to experience *more* clarity and joyful consciousness than ever before.

This happiness will partly be because **heaven is a place of perfection**. 'You have come ... to the assembly of the firstborn who are enrolled in heaven, ... to the spirits of the righteous made perfect.'[10] In Revelation, John relates that the souls of believers in heaven 'were each given a white robe'.[11] Heaven is a spiritual not a material world, but the symbol is one of perfect purity. This is because, as Revelation also explains, 'nothing unclean will ever enter' God's presence in the world to come.[12]

There were times in the army when I spent weeks in the field, emerging afterwards with matted hair, deeply engrained dirt, and

---

of appearance: the person is still and their eyes are closed. The analogy of sleep is also to indicate rest and non-permanence. In other words, in due course, at Christ's return, the sleeper will wake! To push the analogy of sleep beyond these functions, such that heaven is unconscious (a claim known as 'soul sleep'), is to set it against other parts of Scripture and therefore to push it too far.

7. Luke 23:43.
8. Revelation 6:10.
9. 2 Corinthians 12:4.
10. Hebrews 12:22, 23.
11. Revelation 6:11.
12. Revelation 21:27.

smelling like you don't want to know. Afterwards, the long-dreamed-of hot bath and shower and the feeling of fresh, glowing cleanliness was always amazing. Even though we've been wonderfully saved from sin's power and penalty, its presence continues to linger in our lives like clinging, stinking mud.[13] To be finally, totally free of that, after a lifetime of knowing nothing else, will feel extraordinary.

Happiness will also come from the truth that **heaven is a place of reunion**. We will finally be with believing loved ones we may have missed for decades, perhaps to the point of heartbreak. Old Testament writers spoke of dying believers being 'gathered to their people'.[14] David spoke confidently of being reunited with the infant son he lost.[15] Jesus pictures people joyfully welcoming others they recognise into heaven.[16]

If you have lost a parent, friend, spouse or child who was in Christ – even a tiny pre-natal baby – contemplate the truth that you will soon be with them again.[17] Who knows how we will recognise each other in our disembodied state in heaven? It is another world, largely beyond our ability down here to imagine or describe.[18] I suspect that we may sense others' identities and communicate with them not less but *more* fully than we do in our current fallen state.

Yet for all of our rest, consciousness, perfection and reunion, the fundamental cause of heaven's happiness will be **the presence of Jesus**. Paul writes, 'Yet which I shall choose [between living and dying] I cannot tell. I am hard pressed between the two. My desire is to depart *and be with Christ, for that is far better.*'[19] Elsewhere Paul defines heaven as being 'away from the body and *at home with the Lord*'.[20] That is the point of heaven for Paul. We will be in the presence of the Lord from whom rest, consciousness, perfection, and

---

13. 1 John 1:8.

14. Genesis 25:8; 35:29; 49:29; Numbers 20:24; Judges 2:10.

15. 2 Samuel 12:23.

16. Luke 16:9.

17. On the intensely difficult subject of the death of unbelieving loved ones, see the final footnote in Day 26.

18. 1 Corinthians 2:9.

19. Philippians 1:22-23.

20. 2 Corinthians 5:8.

FROM EVERLASTING TO EVERLASTING

all other blessings come. 'You are my Lord; I have no good apart from you.'[21]

We will at long last be with our King, who covenanted to save us, foreknew and elected us, created us in His own image, stooped to become one of us, died for us, rose for us, and then watched over us every step of the way home. We will finally be with the One who, though invisible to us, had been lovingly shepherding us all along. The seventeenth-century Scottish pastor Samuel Rutherford could pray,

> O my Lord Jesus Christ, if I could be in heaven without thee, it would be a hell; and if I could be in hell, and have thee still, it would be a heaven to me, for thou art all the heaven I want.[22]

If we can 'seek the things that are above, where Christ is' and 'set our minds on things that are above, not on things that are on earth,'[23] we will find ourselves encouraged and inspired by the reality awaiting us. We will even be able to say with Paul that were it not for our mission of serving Christ on earth, 'we would rather be away from the body and at home with the Lord'.[24]

Prayer:

Heavenly Father, I praise you for the overwhelming happiness and incomparable rest to which you are leading me. I praise you for the liberating perfection to which I can look forward. I praise you for the longed-for reunions I will experience. But most of all, I praise you that I will finally get to be with the source of these and all other good things, my saviour, master, friend, brother and king. Instead of fearing death, help me to yearn for where it leads. In the name of the One who is seated right now in heaven, Amen.

Meditation:

Has this chapter changed your view of heaven at all? If so, how?

---

21. Psalm 16:2.

22. Samuel Rutherford, *The Loveliness of Christ* ed. Helen Lister (Banner of Truth, 2007), p. 19.

23. Colossians 3:1, 2.

24. 2 Corinthians 5:8.

Day 28
The God Who Resurrects:
The Believer's Resurrection

In 1854, John G. Paton was preparing to go as a missionary to Vanuatu in the South Pacific. Previous missionaries had been murdered within minutes of arriving. Many tried to put Paton off including one man whose crowning argument was 'Cannibals! You will be eaten by cannibals!' Paton's legendary response was this:

> Mr Dickson, you are advanced in years now, and your own prospect is soon to be laid in the grave, there to be eaten by worms; I confess to you, that if I can but live and die serving and honouring the Lord Jesus, it will make no difference to me whether I am eaten by cannibals or by worms; and in the Great Day my resurrection body will arise as fair as yours in the likeness of our risen Redeemer.

The truth of the believer's resurrection comes into focus gradually as the Old Testament progresses. When Sadducees came to Jesus arguing against the resurrection, He reasons that they're wrong because they don't know the Scriptures.[1] He might have had in mind any of the relevant passages in Job, Psalms, Proverbs, Isaiah, Ezekiel and Daniel, not to mention implications of it elsewhere.

The New Testament then holds up the truth of our resurrection particularly as something assured by Jesus' own resurrection.[2] When Paul calls Christ 'the *first*born' from the dead,[3] or the '*first* fruits' of

---

1. Matthew 22:29.

2. 1 Corinthians 6:14; 15:12; 2 Corinthians 4:14.

3. Colossian 1:18.

those of who have died,[4] he is arguing that Christ's resurrection set the precedent and pattern for those who will follow Him. Jesus is our trailblazer.

Liberal theologians down the ages have loved to view the resurrection as merely a metaphor for a spiritual reality. But Jesus made a point of demonstrating just how physical His body was. He ate fish in front of His disciples, probably (as I like to picture Him) with a big grin, smacking His lips with relish.[5] The fact He entered their locked room with apparent ease shows not that He was *less* but if anything *more* physical than the walls! In the world to come, our bodies – along with the rest of the New Creation – can look forward to unfallen, redeemed physicality.

Jesus' own teaching on our resurrection could not have been clearer: 'An hour is coming when all who are in the tombs will hear his voice and come out.'[6] This will happen at Christ's return. 'For the Lord himself will descend from heaven with a cry of command, with the voice of an archangel, and with the sound of the trumpet of God. And the dead in Christ will rise first.'[7]

So whether your body is reduced to a small urn of ashes, buried to decompose in a coffin, used for medical research, harvested for transplants, or meets some other end, it will be re-constituted and raised to life. This might sound outlandish and far-fetched, but consider the words of Bruce Milne:

> If we recall that all that now exists in the universe was brought into being out of nothing by God's power, we are delivered from concern about the 'difficulty' of the general resurrection for an omnipotent God![8]

To those who doubted the general resurrection, Jesus was blunt: 'You are wrong, because you know neither the Scriptures nor the power of God.'[9]

---

4. 1 Corinthians 15:20.

5. John 20:19; Luke 24:36-43.

6. John 5:28, 29.

7. 1 Thessalonians 4:16.

8. Bruce Milne, *Know the Truth: A Handbook of Christian Belief* (IVP, 1982), p. 361.

9. Matthew 22:29.

So consider the current fallenness in your own body. Maybe you find aspects of yourself unsightly or embarrassing. For ten years I had a fungus covering much of my torso and back. Perhaps you're in physical pain even as you read this. Maybe your disfigurement or weight problem or injury or disease overwhelms you at times. (Spoiler for younger readers: things will start to creak at some point, and there is only one direction of travel from there.)

Now turn to consider the truth of your future resurrection. Your body will be raised in flawless beauty and glory. The greatest athlete now would appear clumsy and weak compared to you then. The most beautiful model now would appear plain compared to you then. '[The believer's body] is sown in dishonour; it is raised in glory. It is sown in weakness; it is raised in power.'[10] 'The dead will be raised imperishable, and we shall be changed. For this perishable body must put on the imperishable, and this mortal body must put on immortality.'[11] Andrew Wilson casts a beautiful vision of this:

> Cholera and cancer are consigned to the cosmic skip for all eternity. Operating theatres, doctors, ambulances and health secretaries become a thing of the past. Nobody cries, except for joy. Nobody grieves. The sterile smell of the Emergency Department is no more. The octogenarians, who sit, walnut-faced, under blankets in wheelchairs in hospital reception areas are given a new life and a new youth that will never again be stolen by the long march of time. Every deaf ear is unblocked, every damaged limb is made whole, every blind eye sees. Autism and Down's Syndrome and schizophrenia and Alzheimer's are swallowed up in victory. And the last enemy to be destroyed is death.[12]

The truth of our future resurrection is designed to help us in the present in several ways. For example, it's an encouragement to persevere for Jesus now, no matter what the physical cost. Many believers around the world face hunger, discomfort and physical danger directly because of their faithfulness to Christ. And even in the West, we might be tempted to allow health issues or the struggles of aging to take our focus from Christ. Yet 'the sufferings of this present time are not

---

10. 1 Corinthians 15:43.

11. 1 Corinthians 15:52, 53.

12. Andrew Wilson, *The Life You Never Expected* (IVP, 2015), p. 116.

worth comparing with the glory that is to be revealed to us'.[13] Christ is worth our devotion more than anything, even our own bodies. Don't be discouraged or distracted from Him by your physical demise. Stay the course. It will be so much more than worth it.

The prospect of our resurrection safeguards us from other errors too. On the one hand, some in our world are obsessed with their bodies. Witness the proliferation of cosmetic surgery, muscle supplements, weight-loss drugs, tanning studios, beauty salons, dieting fads, personal trainers, and health magazines. With this outlook, the body is everything.

Others go the opposite way. They trash and neglect their bodies for the sake of food, drink, drugs or other harmful recreations. 'If the dead are not raised, "Let us eat and drink for tomorrow we die."'[14] With this outlook, the body is nothing.

The healthy way to view our bodies, between the extremes of idolising and disrespecting, between obsession and neglect, is revealed by the truth of the resurrection:

On the one hand, our bodies are not everything. Jesus Christ is everything. And it is He who will one day raise them from inevitable decay to permanent perfection. The best thing for our bodies is therefore, counter-intuitively, to live *not* for them but for Him. 'For while bodily training is of some value, godliness is of value in every way, as it holds promise for the present life and also for the life to come.'[15]

Equally, our bodies are not nothing. God designed them and cares about them, which gives them value. 'You knitted me together in my mother's womb. I praise you, for I am fearfully and wonderfully made. Wonderful are your works.'[16] Our Maker will be pleased one day to raise His handiwork for His glory. To trash or neglect it is to dishonour Him. Instead we can know that as we 'nourish and cherish our own flesh'[17] appropriately, we honour the One behind it.

---

13. Romans 8:18.
14. 1 Corinthians 15:32.
15. 1 Timothy 4:8.
16. Psalm 139:13, 14.
17. Ephesians 5:29.

'For I know that my Redeemer lives, and at the last he will stand upon the earth. And after my skin has been thus destroyed, yet in my flesh I shall see God.'[18]

Prayer:

Loving Creator, thank you for your promise to restore and perfect this fallen body from which I am praying to you at this moment. I praise you for creating it and soon re-creating it. Help me to honour you by cultivating a healthy relationship with it, neither idolising nor disrespecting it. Help me to use it well in your service in this life, and to enjoy it. And help me to look forward to when I can glorify you from a body with unimaginable beauty and energy. In the name of the One who gave His body for mine, Amen.

Meditation:

What do you like most and least about your body? How do the truths discussed in this chapter affect the way you view your body?

18. Job 19:25, 26.

Day 29

The God Who Holds Accountable:
The Believer's Judgement

One of the sharper prods the Bible has administered to me over the years was the truth of the believer's judgement. My father explained it one morning at our breakfast family devotion. He was gentle and understated but the Holy Spirit wasn't. I was a spiritually smug little antinomian who thought I had the Christian faith nailed. I had ticked the box to receive eternal fire insurance and was now comfortably set for a life of coasting for Jesus. I still remember my complacence evaporating as the reality of the believer's judgement dawned on me. Here's how Paul articulates it:

> We [Christians] must all appear before the judgment seat of Christ, so that each one may receive what is due for what he has done in the body, whether good or evil.[1]

We are saved by faith alone and not by works. Yet, as I learned that day over untouched porridge, we will nonetheless be held accountable by God for every one of our actions in this life, both good and bad.[2] What's more, we will experience consequences for them. Had I been spiritually healthier, I would have registered that this doctrine isn't designed only to warn and hold to account those looking for self-serving shortcuts in the Christian life. It also serves to encourage and inspire believers who are serving Christ faithfully.

---

1. 2 Corinthians 5:10.

2. Romans 14:10-12; 2 Corinthians 5:10; Matthew 6:1-6, 16, 18; Matthew 10:41, 42; Revelation 22:12.

Walk with me through another example of the Bible's teaching on this, from 1 Corinthians 3:

> Now if anyone builds on the foundation with gold, silver, precious stones, wood, hay, straw – each one's work will become manifest, for the Day will disclose it, because it will be revealed by fire, and the fire will test what sort of work each one has done.[3]

In context, the 'foundation' mentioned here is Jesus Christ and 'building on it' refers to the service of others, particularly by leaders but by extension all believers.[4] Gold, silver and precious stones picture valuable, beautiful, authentic service, and wood, hay and straw stand for shoddy, low quality, worthless service. These two types of service can appear indistinguishable to the human eye in this world, but the truth will out. That will happen on what Paul calls 'the Day', or elsewhere 'the Day of the Lord', Christ's return. The fire mentioned is God's revealing, testing scrutiny.

Paul continues in 1 Corinthians 3, 'If the work that anyone has built on the foundation survives, he will receive a reward.'[5] This reward can't merely refer to salvation, because the next verse contrasts it with the cowboy builders of the Christian life who instead suffer loss, yet are still saved: 'If anyone's work is burned up, he will suffer loss [the loss of the reward], though he himself will be saved, but only as through fire.'[6]

I've known some Christians be nervous over the idea of varying rewards, perhaps because of the relational dynamics they imagine resulting in the New Creation. However, we will feel no resentment or envy or insecurity or regret when others receive greater rewards than us, nor pity or embarrassment towards others who receive lesser. Our existence will be utterly devoid of sin or sadness. We will all be maximally fulfilled and joyful, even if individuals' maximums vary.

The parable of the ten minas in Luke 19 indicates that levels of rewards will vary to reflect our levels of faithfulness.[7] The servant who

---

3. 1 Corinthians 3:12, 13.

4. For this principle applying directly to all believers, see 1 Corinthians 12:7, 12-31; 14:12.

5. 1 Corinthians 3:14.

6. 1 Corinthians 3:15.

7. Luke 19:11-27.

invested his master's assets the most faithfully received the greatest reward: 'I will set you over ten cities.' The next servant, with less to show for his efforts, heard 'you are to be over five cities'. A similar picture emerges from the parable of the talents in Matthew 25, as well as elsewhere in the New Testament.[8]

Some believers can be worried about the notion of merit-based rewards because our salvation is unrelated to our merit. We must of course guard the truth that we are saved only by grace. Yet that is not at stake here. Here we are talking about believers' experience in eternity *following* their receipt of salvation. In each of the parables of the minas and talents, the third servant not only fails to receive a reward. He fails to be saved. This is not because he didn't earn enough merit, but because his lack of service exposed his heart.[9] He had never been transformed by grace in the first place.

In any case, receiving rewards from God for our obedience doesn't undermine grace. It promotes it! As Augustine of Hippo observed, 'When God crowns your merits [with rewards], he is not crowning anything but his own gifts.'[10] We receive rewards because of obedience which God Himself empowered in us. As Augustine famously prayed, 'Command what you will; grant what you command.'[11]

Despite this, might it still be somehow morally wrong or cynical to be motivated to serve Christ by these rewards? God's Word says not. In fact, it holds out such rewards for precisely that function. The key

---

8. Another passage is Romans 14:10-12. The New Testament also uses the language of 'reward' for believers frequently. Sometimes the context indicates that the reward is salvation. However, on other occasions the context means that this meaning of 'reward' seems to make little sense. In these cases, Christians are urged to serve *more* faithfully, or work *harder*, or endure *greater* suffering on the basis that resulting rewards make their (*more* faithful) service worthwhile.

9. James 2:14-17 makes this principle jarringly clear: 'What good is it, my brothers, if someone says he has faith but does not have works? Can that faith save him? If a brother or sister is poorly clothed and lacking in daily food, and one of you says to them, "Go in peace, be warmed and filled," without giving them the things needed for the body, what good is that? So also faith by itself, if it does not have works, is dead.'

10. Augustine, Sermons, trans. Edmund Hill, in *The Works of Saint Augustine: A Translation for the 21st Century,* ed. John E. Rotelle, part 3, vols. 1–11 (Brooklyn, NY: New City Press, 1990), 333.2,5.

11. *The Confessions of St. Augustine*, Book 9, Chapter 29.

is understanding them rightly. Ultimately, rewards don't represent a different motivation for faithfulness than any other the Bible puts forward: God's glory. We pursue our own happiness in Him because that glorifies Him, and these rewards from His hand will heighten our happiness. The bestowal of these rewards and our eternal enjoyment of them only redounds to God's greater glory.

What will these future rewards look like? Scripture has little to say about this, perhaps to encourage us to get on with storing them up instead of idly speculating about them. In any case, I take it that our fallen minds and limited imaginations wouldn't be able to cope with the glorious realities ahead of us. 'What no eye has seen, nor ear heard, nor the heart of man imagined, what God has prepared for those who love him.'[12]

That said, we are given glimpses. In Luke 19, the rewards take the form of being set over cities. In Matthew 25, they take the form of being 'set over much'.[13] It seems that the more faithful we are in this life, the more authority and responsibility we'll be given in the life to come. Such leadership won't lead to stress or discomfort as it can in this world. In that world, it will only lead to even deeper fulfilment and joy.

Perhaps rewards might also take the form simply of intensified experiences of the New Creation's other characteristics (See Day 30): greater proximity to God somehow, more joy, greater appreciation of beauty, a more gifted body, more intimate relationships with others, more privileged service opportunities. Who knows! Every single human in that world will be flawlessly happy, happier than our wildest dreams could possibly capture now. Yet there will be varying rewards. The point is to get on now with serving Jesus as faithfully as we can so as to receive them!

One day you will stand before your Lord and Saviour and He will scrutinise your service of Him. Don't settle for drifting through the Christian life as one of those lukewarm, guilt-ridden, joyless drudges – one of those Christians who try and get away with the bare minimum of service that validates their faith as genuine, and squeak into heaven

12. 1 Corinthians 2:9.
13. Matthew 25:21, 23.

'but only as one escaping through the flames'.[14] That's a dangerous game to play. Many are the souls who thought to settle for the easy option of being the second servant instead of the first – but realised to their horror, after they had died, that they had in fact been the third servant all along.

Instead, push hard, all the way home, crying out to God for more grace to empower more obedience. And do so knowing that you're gaining rewards beyond what your heart can now imagine. They are rewards which your loving Father will one day bestow on you with overflowing joy, to the praise of His grace and for His greater glory.

Let this doctrine be the wind in your sails that God intends.

Prayer:

God of grace, I praise you for the wise and loving spur you place before me of the believer's judgement. Would its prospect help steer me away from self-serving shortcuts in the Christian life, and instead towards whole-hearted, joyful, urgent commitment to Jesus. Help me to serve you now so that you can bless me then with glorious rewards, for my increased joy and your increased glory. In the name of the One who for the joy set before Him was faithful even unto death, Amen.

Meditation:

How do you feel about God's assessment of your actions at the end of your life? Why?

---

14. 1 Corinthians 3:15 (NIV).

Day 30
The God Who Renews: The New Creation

Think back to some of the most joyful moments in your life.

Maybe they include discovering your stocking on Christmas morning as a child, or setting off on a once-in-a-lifetime holiday with friends. The truth is that our experiences of happiness in this life, even at their best, are faint echoes of a reality yet to come, far beyond anything we can conceive. 'What no eye has seen, nor ear heard, nor the heart of man imagined, what God has prepared for those who love him.'[1]

Our journey which began with God's Eternal Covenant in eternity past, will finally reach its consummation in eternity future, as He renews creation. 'He who was seated on the throne said, "Behold, I am making all things new."'[2] 'I create new heavens and a new earth, and the former things shall not be remembered or come into mind. But be glad and rejoice forever in that which I create.'[3] We can sum up the nature of this New Creation with seven 'P's:

The supreme characteristic will be the **presence of God**. God is of course omnipresent now and always has been. Yet Scripture describes His presence then in a special, unprecedented way. 'We shall see him as he is.'[4] 'They will see his face.'[5] 'Behold, the dwelling place of God

---

1. 1 Corinthians 2:9.
2. Revelation 21:5.
3. Isaiah 65:17, 18.
4. 1 John 3:2.
5. Revelation 22:4.

is *with man*. He will dwell *with them*, and they will be his people, and God himself will be *with them* as their God.'[6]

In Bruce Milne's words, 'The crowning wonder of our experience ... will be the endless exploration of that unutterable beauty, majesty, love, holiness, power, joy and grace which is God himself.'[7]

Because of God's presence, the New Creation will be characterised by **perfect joy and beauty.**

> He will wipe away every tear from their eyes, and death shall be no more, neither shall there be mourning, nor crying, nor pain anymore, for the former things have passed away.[8]

Jonathan Edwards said that God's love is like 'an ocean without shores or bottom'.[9] The same is true of all His virtues, and we will spend eternity swimming and diving in that ocean, consumed with joy and worship.

Human language creaks under the weight of trying to describe this coming reality. Paul talks of creation groaning now for the time it will be 'set free from its bondage to corruption'.[10] Isaiah describes how 'the earth shall be full of the knowledge of the LORD as the waters cover the sea'.[11] When this universe is finally liberated from the incalculable effects of the Fall, what will the mountains and the oceans and the galaxy look like? What enhanced human interactions with the animal and plant kingdoms will be possible?

Part of this New Creation will be our own perfected and glorified **physical bodies.**

> [The human body] is sown in dishonour; it is raised in glory. It is sown in weakness; it is raised in power. It is sown a natural body; it is raised a spiritual body ... Just as we have borne the image of

---

6. Revelation 21:3.

7. Bruce Milne, *Know the Truth: A Handbook of Christian Belief* (IVP, 1982), p. 340.

8. Revelation 21:4.

9. Jonathan Edwards, 'That God is the Father of Lights' in *The Blessing of God: Previously Unpublished Sermons of Jonathan Edwards*, ed. Michael McMullen (Broadman, 2003), p. 350.

10. Romans 8:21, 22.

11. Isaiah 11:9.

the man of dust [Adam], we shall also bear the image of the man of heaven [Christ].[12]

How fast will we be able to run? How deep will we be able to swim? What will it be like never again to feel physical tiredness or pain, at least not unpleasantly? What new powers of taste, or smell, or hearing, or sight, or touch, or mental ability, or even previously unutilised modes of perception will we be capable of?

And in the presence of God, with undreamed-of happiness and beauty all around us and glorified physical bodies, we'll also enjoy **personal relationships.** Scripture gives multiple indications of rich, fulfilling relationships in the life to come.[13]

In Revelation, John describes a great wedding feast.[14] Picture the best party you can imagine: beaming smiles and infectious laughter, joyful reunions and embraces, blossoming friendships, exuberant dancing, the fascination of getting to know new people and the fulfilment of getting to be known by them. The crippling loneliness for many in this world will vanish forever and be replaced with more rewarding friendships than any currently in existence.

Relationships will be on a different plane from any in this world. No one will be irritable or hard to love. Everyone's personalities, while beautifully unique, will also radiate Christ-like beauty. There will be no misunderstandings, disappointments, quarrels or impatience. There won't even be theological disagreements as Jesus' prayer for His people's unity is finally fulfilled.[15]

The New Creation will also be a place of **privileged responsibilities.** Increased faithfulness in this world will lead to increased rewards in the world to come. In Luke 19, Jesus pictures these rewards as positions of authority over cities.[16] In Matthew 25, he envisions servants who are 'set ... over much'.[17]

---

12. 1 Corinthians 15:43, 44, 49.

13. See 'Day 27. The God Who Receives: Heaven'.

14. Revelation 19:9.

15. Jeremiah 31:34; John 17:21.

16. Luke 19:11-27.

17. Matthew 25:14-30.

It is hard to know exactly what these honoured roles will look like, but we can be confident that none of us will experience envy or resentment towards others who receive them. After all, we will be sinless. We will simply rejoice for those others. Equally, major responsibilities in the New Creation won't cause stress or anxiety for those of *us* receiving them. Our own perfection and God's empowerment of us will mean that we feel only deeper fulfilment and joy.

As well as this, we will engage in **practical service**. Human work is fundamentally good and existed in the perfect, pre-Fall world. It was only cursed when sin entered the world.[18] What will work look like when, as John says in Revelation, 'no longer will there be anything accursed'?[19] Describing the New Creation, Isaiah says 'They shall build houses and inhabit them; they shall plant vineyards and eat their fruit … My chosen shall long enjoy the work of their hands. They shall not labour in vain.'[20]

Revelation speaks of us serving God, and of the glory and honour of the nations being brought into God's city.[21] This would seem to describe the best of human culture – art, music, literature, technology, science, cuisine, exploration, sport, and so on. Wayne Grudem pictures us working 'at the whole range of the investigation and development of creation by technological [and] creative … means'.[22] What new art works, symphonies, novels, inventions, discoveries, recipes, athletic feats, and even space colonisation might we engage in for God's glory?

Finally, the New Creation will be characterised by **perpetual time**. It seems likely that instead of being timeless, the New Creation will be characterised by an unending succession of moments. The Bible's descriptions to us of the world to come involve sequences of events such as speaking words one after another. Revelation pictures the tree of life 'yielding its fruit *each month*'.[23] And while one of God's essential attributes is His ex-temporality – His freedom from the time

---

18. Genesis 3:16-19.

19. Revelation 22:3.

20. Isaiah 65:21, 22, 23.

21. Revelation 21:5, 24-26.

22. Wayne Grudem, *Systematic Theology: An Introduction to Biblical Doctrine* (IVP, 1994), p. 1162.

23. Revelation 22:2.

He created – we are finite creatures who don't by nature share such attributes. And so, in the words of Edward Donnelly, 'At moments of utter happiness, a voice inside us whispers, "I want this to go on forever." In heaven it will!'[24]

Whatever the difficulty of your Christian walk right now, or your disappointment at the way your life has turned out, keep going. It will all be worth it. Paul said it well: 'For I consider that the sufferings of this present time *are not worth comparing* with the glory that is to be revealed to us.'[25]

See you there.

Prayer:

Lord of heaven and earth, I praise you for one day making all things new. Thank you for leading me home, step by step, from the Covenant of Redemption in eternity past to the New Creation in eternity future. Thank you for your loving command to me to 'set your hope fully on the grace that will be brought to you at the revelation of Jesus Christ'.[26] Help me to do that with joy and confidence for the rest of my days on this earth. In the name of the One by whom I will enjoy your New Creation, Amen.

Meditation:

What do you most look forward to about the New Creation? Why?

---

24. Edward Donnelly, *Heaven and Hell* (Banner of Truth, 2001), p. 126.

25. Romans 8:18.

26. 1 Peter 1:13.

Christian Focus Publications

Our mission statement —

STAYING FAITHFUL
In dependence upon God we seek to impact the world through
literature faithful to His infallible Word, the Bible. Our aim is
to ensure that the Lord Jesus Christ is presented as the only hope
to obtain forgiveness of sin, live a useful life and look forward to
heaven with Him.

Our books are published in four imprints:

CHRISTIAN
FOCUS

Popular works including biographies,
commentaries, basic doctrine and
Christian living.

CHRISTIAN
HERITAGE

Books representing some of
the best material from the rich
heritage of the church.

MENTOR

Books written at a level suitable
for Bible College and seminary
students, pastors, and other serious
readers. The imprint includes
commentaries, doctrinal studies,
examination of current issues and
church history.

CF4•K

Children's books for quality Bible
teaching and for all age groups:
Sunday school curriculum, puzzle and
activity books; personal and family
devotional titles, biographies and
inspirational stories – because you are
never too young to know Jesus!

Christian Focus Publications Ltd,
Geanies House, Fearn, Ross-shire,
IV20 1TW, Scotland, United Kingdom.
www.christianfocus.com
blog.christianfocus.com